TO

_____

FROM

_____

DATE

_____

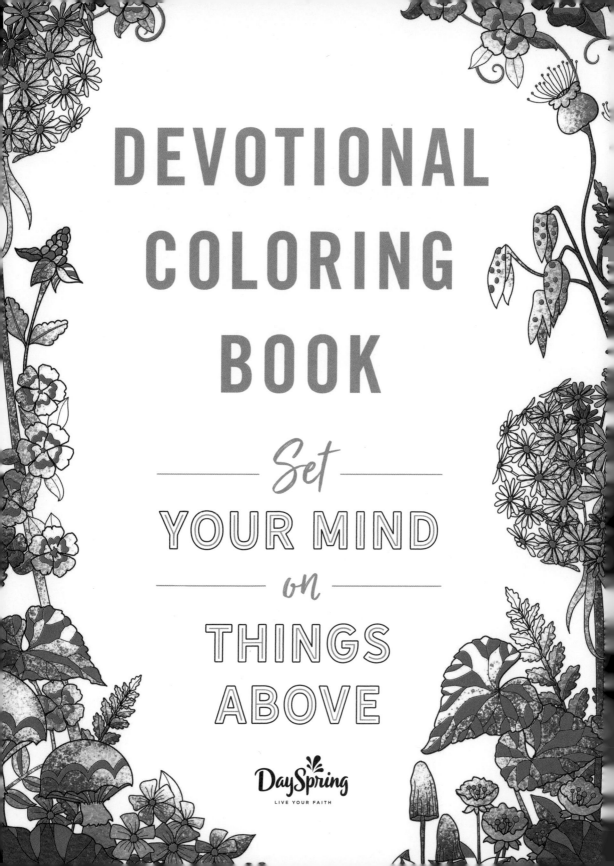

DEVOTIONAL COLORING BOOK

Set
YOUR MIND
on
THINGS ABOVE

DaySpring
LIVE YOUR FAITH

When the Bible tells us to "set [our] minds on things above, not on earthly things" (Colossians 3:2 NIV), we aren't being told to neglect the earth or ignore the beauty there. Setting our minds on things above means looking at everyday, ordinary things like flowers, seashells, ocean waves, gardens, and relationships through the lens of heaven. How can the ocean waves soothe our souls? What do flowers tell us about our great Creator? How do the earthly things build our appreciation for the One who made them?

As you read these devotions and fill in the coloring pages, let them elevate your thoughts to God. Coloring calms the mind, leaving it prepared for the messages of hope in each devotion. Together they set a pattern of thinking, a calm centeredness that shuts out the distraction of earthly things.

Read, color, pray, and set your mind on better things.

REFLECTIONS

*Only in returning to Me and
resting in Me will you be saved.
In quietness and confidence is your strength.*

ISAIAH 30:15 NLT

Have you been on a body of water when no breeze is blowing? When the only the sound is insects stirring the thick summer air? When the languid water and hazy blue sky pose as mirrors, the image and colors of the heavens reflecting so perfectly on the still water that it can't be discerned where one ends and the other begins. It's a palette of blues in differing hues, dotted by clouds. But as fish or bugs break the surface and ripples roll across the surface, the illusion is lost.

The truth is, reflections are seen best in the stillness. It is why God calls out to His very busy creatures to "be still, and know that I am God" (Psalm 46:10 NIV). While we carry on the frantic pace of our lives, we miss the beauty of all that is above. We worry, we stress, we plan, we manipulate, we labor long to make life work the way we think it should, when all along we'd be better off being still and reflecting the beauty of the life God has given us.

Today, take time to be still. Sit in silence before the God who made you and knows you. Listen for the still, small Voice that tells you what your heart really needs to know for this day. When you take time to sit still in God's glorious presence, you take on His image—a work of beauty that will take the world's breath away.

LORD, THANK YOU FOR THE BEAUTY OF REFLECTIONS. STILL MY HEART AND SOUL SO THAT I BECOME A BETTER REFLECTION OF YOU.

COLORING LOVE

God looked over everything He had made;
it was so good, so very good!

GENESIS 1:31 THE MESSAGE

Do you remember the first time you opened a box of crayons? The smell of wax and paper tightly wrapped around each beautiful color arrested the senses and set imagination to flight. In an instant you were an artist, transforming the ordinary white sheet of paper before you into lines and shapes and patterns that washed your world with color right before your eyes. What were stick figures and circular flowers to older, less-sensitive souls were your early masterpieces, your version of Eden.

But what if, instead of a full spectrum of differing hues, your box had only one color? It may have entertained you for a moment but certainly wouldn't have held your attention. There's beauty in diversity and pleasure in harmony. We witness the same miracle every time we open our eyes and truly see the world around us. God did not make our world a monochromatic experience. Brilliant color fills the skies, the trees, and the land, if we will just look up. Eyes and skin and cars and houses and flowers and oceans all treat our eyes to a feast of colors that turn the entire world into an extraordinary work of art. Recapture the wonder of color as you get ready for the day. Notice the hues in everything your hands touch and your eyes view. Then give thanks to the One who prized you enough to color your world with His creativity and love, making your brilliant, beautiful life into an integral part of His magnificent masterpiece.

LORD, THANK YOU FOR ALL THE COLORS IN THE WORLD. THEY DELIGHT MY EYES AND INSPIRE MY CREATIVITY!

FIX YOUR THOUGHTS

Quiet down before GOD, be prayerful before Him.

PSALM 37:7 THE MESSAGE

When we're encouraged to quiet down before God and be prayerful, there's a good chance it isn't our voice we need to silence, but our mind. That's where the trouble starts as far as worry, anxiety, and fear are concerned. Thoughts send chain reactions through our bodies—both good and bad ones. That's why Paul said to "Fix your thoughts on what is true and good and right. Think about things that are pure and lovely" (Philippians 4:8 TLB). Paul understood the mind-body connection, and he knew our worries and fears could cause us to fold under pressure.

If we start to believe things contrary to God's love and truth, anxiety can establish a pathway to destroy our overall well-being. Getting our minds to quiet down before God begins with filling them up with what His Word says: "Truly my soul finds rest in God" (Psalm 62:1 NIV); "Return to your rest, my soul, for the LORD has been good to you" (Psalm 116:7 NIV); "Come to Me, all you who are weary and burdened, and I will give you rest" (Matthew 11:28 NIV). Rooting out negativity will get us to a place of relaxing in God's faithfulness. The quicker we pluck out the lies, the faster the quiet comes and the sooner we get to the second part of Psalm 37:7 THE MESSAGE, "Be prayerful before Him." Prayer brings the best rest to every part of us. In prayer, we have God's ear and we learn His heart. It's a conversation that invites us to tap into our lifeline. It is a beautiful thing to give our spirit, soul, and body the rest it needs.

FATHER, GIVE ME STRENGTH AND WISDOM TO REMOVE THE NEGATIVITY IN MY MIND, CLEARING THE PATH FOR PEACE, REST, AND A RENEWED CONFIDENCE IN YOU.

WHAT ABOUT ME?

Therefore, encourage one another and build one another up, just as you also are doing.

I THESSALONIANS 5:11 NASB

Paul makes it very clear in I Thessalonians that we are to encourage and build up one another. One would think that would be the easiest thing in the world to do—especially when it comes to encouraging those we love. But sadly, for many, encouraging words just don't roll off the tongue.

We live in a social-media-saturated world that seems to scream, "What about *me*?" And while social-media platforms can be used to connect believers, send out prayer requests, and share news with friends and family, it can also set the stage for self-centeredness. Self-centeredness makes it difficult to be happy for someone else's success while struggling to find our own. Online media directs our focus to ourselves, while the encouragement Paul describes focuses on serving others: "Therefore encourage one another and build one another up." The funny thing about encouragement is that the more you encourage someone else, the more you feel encouraged. It's beautiful how that works, isn't it? And it's also God's way.

What would happen if we spent more time focusing on encouraging and building up one another than emphasizing self: changing our "What about me?" to "What about others?" Or what if we asked God for direction and guidance so that He could give us the words and actions needed to encourage the people placed on our paths?

JESUS, HELP ME ENCOURAGE OTHERS AND BUILD THEM UP, JUST AS YOU HAVE ALWAYS DONE. THANK YOU FOR BEING MY EXAMPLE.

WANTING WISDOM

If you need wisdom, ask our generous God,
and He will give it to you.
He will not rebuke you for asking.

JAMES 1:5 NLT

As children mature, they face life-changing decisions. Do they go to college? Which college? What career path? Where should they live? How do they pay for it? These are just a few of the questions they grapple with. But it doesn't end there. They'll need to know where to move once their degree is completed. And if and who they should marry. Children or no children? Natural or adoption? Be a stay-at-home parent or balance family and workplace?

And it seems it's not just the young men and women who need wisdom. The older we get, the more we realize just how many choices come with each new day. Fortunately, we know Someone who has the answers we need and the divine perspective we lack. God, who knows the end of the story before it begins, sees exactly what is best for our lives. Every ounce of wisdom we need for today can be found in Him and His Word. In fact, God invites us to bring it on. No matter what we've done in the past, God promises not to condemn us when we come to Him and ask for help. Instead, He pours His wisdom—the divine kind—into our lives. Life may throw us a thousand curve balls, but God, with His eternal perspective and insight, is the expert on hitting each one out of the park. This morning, ask Him to give you the wisdom you need to know, and follow His path.

> LORD, GIVE ME THE WISDOM I NEED TO FOLLOW YOU. DEVELOP IN ME GOOD JUDGMENT.

WHAT IS LIFE ALL ABOUT?

There's nothing better to do than go ahead and . . .

get the most we can out of life . . . It's God's gift.

ECCLESIASTES 3:12–13 THE MESSAGE

You've probably heard someone respond to a disappointing outcome by saying, "That's life." Makes it sound like life is something to be endured rather than lived, doesn't it? On the other hand, you've probably heard someone say, "Life is beautiful," and you wonder whether that person has a taxing job as you do or bills to pay and a family to take care of. In fact, life consists of both these perspectives and much more.

Life is God's gift, but He hasn't left you to navigate its wonders and difficulties on your own. He's given you an instruction manual to go with it. The commandments and principles laid out in the Bible are not intended to condemn you or send you chasing after some unattainable standard. God designed them to help you get the most out of life—one moment, hour, and day at a time.

In addition to the precious gift of life He's given and the instruction manual that goes with it, God has promised to walk through each new day with you. Together you will discover what life is all about.

FATHER GOD, THANK YOU FOR GIVING ME LIFE. EVEN WHEN I AM GOING THROUGH DIFFICULT TIMES, I REALIZE THE WONDER OF BEING ALIVE. HELP ME AS I APPLY THE PRINCIPLES IN THE BIBLE TO THE ISSUES IN MY LIFE. AMEN.

THERE'S NOTHING
BETTER TO DO
THAN GO AHEAD
AND...
GET THE MOST
WE CAN
OUT OF LIFE...

It's God's gift.

ECCLESIASTES 3:12–13
THE MESSAGE

HUES OF HOPE

When Jesus woke up, He rebuked the wind
and said to the waves, "Silence! Be still!"
Suddenly the wind stopped, and there was a great calm.

MARK 4:39 NLT

The storm's severity caught you off guard. Though you could see the dark clouds looming as you drove across town, you had no idea how fast and hard the rain could fall. So you pulled off to the side of the road, deciding to wait it out. As suddenly as it started, it stopped. The clouds pushed past and the sun came streaming through crystal-blue skies. But before you could start out on the road, curiosity caused you to turn and look. There it was—a rainbow shining brighter than the sun's rays on rain-soaked streets, painting the dark sky behind with an amazing palette of color.

Is it any wonder that God chose a rainbow to promise hope to Noah and his family after such a horrific flood? Rainbows are God's colorful reminders that there is no storm in our lives so strong or too dark that God can't create something beautiful out of it.

What storms—if any—loom on your horizon? Even if one takes you by surprise, you do not need to be afraid. Just as Jesus stilled the waves and calmed the storms for His disciples, God also has the power to carry you through whatever the day brings. The light of His presence packs a remarkable power to shine through our moments and reveal a beauty we never thought possible. Storms are simply our invitation to trust Him as He works miracles into every moment.

> LORD, NO MATTER HOW THE WIND BLOWS, LET ME ALWAYS LOOK TO YOU FOR DIRECTION. YOU ARE THE WEATHERVANE THAT KEEPS POINTING ME IN THE RIGHT DIRECTION.

THE WAY IN WHICH WE SHOULD GO

Thy word is a lamp unto my feet,

and a light unto my path.

PSALM 119:105 KJV

An estimated two to three million visitors hike portions of America's 2,181-mile Appalachian Trail each year. Hailed as the longest continuously marked footpath in the world, the Appalachian Trail is easily identified, with a marker about every seventy feet, and well-maintained—but it is still easy to get lost there. A stop for a bathroom break or just to rest is all it takes for a tired soul to get turned around and lose their way. Yearly, there are dozens of stories about people who have gotten lost on the trail.

With God as our Guide, we will always succeed in reaching our destination. The only way to completely fail is to ignore our Guide and the trail markers of God's Word. Choosing our own path is the way of destruction. Some people get lost or in trouble when they start out on the right path but decide to take a detour or two. Others get lost because of inattention or distraction. God in His tender mercy never abandons those who are lost and want to find their way back. He goes to them and guides them to the right path. He is never far away from those with repentant hearts.

JESUS, HELP ME TO STAY CLOSE BEHIND YOU AND SET MY FEET IN YOUR FOOTPRINTS. ILLUMINATE THE PATH BEFORE ME AND ENCOURAGE ME TO STAY ON IT.

DON'T GET YOUR FEATHERS RUFFLED!

Everyone will share the story of Your wonderful goodness; they will sing with joy about Your righteousness. The LORD is merciful and compassionate, slow to get angry and filled with unfailing love. The LORD is good to everyone. He showers compassion on all His creation.

PSALM 145:7–9 NLT

If you have ever seen a geyser blow, then you know that it is quite a memorable sight. Seeing that spewing eruption may remind you of someone you know with a cantankerous constitution. Everybody knows somebody like that, right? At work, in your family, in your child's playgroup, a friend or two, a checker at the grocery store, or someone at church . . . or maybe it's you! When that person gets their feathers ruffled, well, they might get quiet and red-faced for a moment, but then you'll want to step back—they're going to blow!

The earth has plenty of those boiling-cauldron-style temperaments, which doesn't make for a lot of goodwill toward men. But we can rest assured that God isn't like that. The Lord is slow to anger. He does not have the frail and fallen nature of humanity, which is riddled with self-interest and poor judgment. God instead shows us love that is steadfast and everlasting. In fact, the Lord showers kindness on all He has created—including you. When we do get our feathers ruffled, may we drown out the outbursts with praises to God. May we tell of His goodness and mercy. May we allow His Spirit to flood our souls with His goodness so that, if people do find us gushing, it will be with God's radiant praise!

DEAREST JESUS, YOU KNOW THAT FROM TIME TO TIME I LET MY TEMPER GET THE BEST OF ME. PLEASE FLOOD MY SOUL WITH YOUR PATIENCE AND MERCY AND PRAISE FOR YOUR GOODNESS!

GOD'S HEART OVERFLOWS

He escorts me to the banquet hall;

it's obvious how much he loves me.

SONG OF SOLOMAN 2:4 NLT

If you feel there's a deficit of love in your life, you aren't alone. When it comes to this greatest of human needs, a worldwide famine is raging. Parents abandon their children to selfishly indulge in drugs and alcohol, children rebel against their parents and take advantage of their elders, husbands and wives wage war, and friends come and go. Where can anyone find deep and satisfying love?

The Scriptures say that God is the essence, fulfillment, and source of love. His love is strong and resilient, forgiving and boundless. No matter how many come to Him, there is more than enough for all. God's love is truly a feast in the wilderness. Best of all, God's love is a gift. All He asks is that you allow Him to fill your heart to overflowing so you can share His bounty with others.

Human love can never fully satisfy the love-starved heart. Only when it's mingled with God's love can it stand the test of time. God wants to love you as you've never been loved before, and He has invited you to His banquet table. Will you come?

FATHER GOD, THANK YOU FOR LOVE THAT IS MORE THAN ENOUGH TO SATISFY MY HUNGRY HEART. YOUR LOVE STRENGTHENS AND HEALS ME. IT MAKES ME LONG TO SHARE IT WITH OTHERS. THANK YOU FOR WELCOMING ME AT YOUR TABLE. AMEN.

BUT GOD

What is impossible with man
is possible with God.

LUKE 18:27 ESV

You've prayed and searched God's Word and asked your friends and your church to pray, but the thing you expected God to do hasn't happened. You've come to the end of your hope. Is it time to give up? To accept that the answer is no?

Soon after the apostle James was beheaded, Peter was thrown into prison, bound in chains between two soldiers, with sentries guarding the door (Acts 12:6). His situation looked hopeless. Peter was probably thinking, *I guess I'm next.* But God sent an angel that night, and the heavy chains fell off his hands. The doors opened and Peter walked out.

The minor prophet Habakkuk grew impatient while waiting for an answer to his prayers. "How long, Lord, must I call for help, but You do not listen?" (Habakkuk 1:2 NIV). Your situation might look just as hopeless, beyond restoration, or completely past help. But God. When you are caught in the teeth of an impossible situation and there is no way out, God is your only plan. "Without faith it is impossible to please him, for whoever would draw near to God must believe that he exists and that he rewards those who seek him" (Hebrews 11:6 ESV). Pray. Wait without worrying and you will see the Lord work in His perfect timing.

LORD, HELP ME TO SEEK THE KINGDOM OF GOD AND YOUR RIGHTEOUSNESS EVEN IN MY WAITING. INCREASE MY FAITH AND DECREASE MY FEAR. I TRUST YOU. HELP ME CLING TO THAT TRUST.

UNIQUELY YOU

He who began a good work in you
will bring it to completion
at the day of Jesus Christ.

PHILIPPIANS 1:6 ESV

If you've sat in church pews long enough over the years, you've heard a lot of people sing a lot of songs. Sometimes the same songs. And you start to realize that ten people can sing the same song, but they won't sing it the same way. The person who was born with the right voice to sing a particular song will sing it to perfection. They will sing with their whole heart, with their very soul. God created each of us for something special but we may spend half our lives piddling around doing many other things rather than answering the call of the thing God meant for us.

It's easy to talk ourselves out of doing what our heart nudges us toward. We convince ourselves that we can't, that we're not good enough, that it's impossible for however many reasons. Has God called you to the missionary field? To write a book? To the ministry? To sing? Then do it. You might not be very good at it at first, but with God's help, you will be. Surrender your doubts, your fears, and your insecurities to God and answer the call to your life's work, whatever it may be. God can create an extraordinary work in your hands that would be an ordinary work in someone else's.

FATHER, THANK YOU FOR CREATING ME UNIQUE AND SPECIAL, FOR A PURPOSE AND A REASON, DESIGNED TO PRODUCE THE MAXIMUM RESULTS FROM MY GIFTS, TALENTS, AND WILLING HEART.

GONE FISHING

Jesus called out to them, "Come, follow Me!
And I will make you fishermen for the souls of men!"

MARK 1:17 TLB

Are you a fisherman or -woman? Have you taken your family fishing? Outfitting yourself for the day can be overwhelming. There is an umpteen number of fishing-rod options along with an entire wall of lures and jigs that all promise success. Of course there's always the live bait—which seems to be of particular interest to children of a certain age. Once you purchase the day's entertainment, you pray hard that at least one person will catch something.

But in fishing, there are potential pitfalls—weeds to the left and low-hanging branches to the right . . . inexperienced fishermen chomping at the bit to get their big worms on small hooks . . . . Though lines tangle and minnows steal the bait, eventually most people catch something, even if it is of miniature size. The experience leaves us feeling grateful for the success and the memories.

Jesus compared faith-sharing to fishing. Of course, He was talking to some real-life fishermen who could easily understand the connection, but the analogy isn't lost on us either. Sharing our faith can be daunting, but God tells us not to worry. Witnessing isn't setting a hook; it's sharing your story. The lure to hearers is actually God's Spirit, who brings in the catch when He's ready. We simply make the effort to drop a line by talking to others about what God has done. Ask God to help you fish for people. Ask Him to place on your heart those who need to hear His encouraging words, and bait your conversation with the beauty of God's love.

JESUS, USE ME AS BAIT TO HOOK THE UNSAVED ON YOUR LOVE AND SALVATION. REVEAL TO ME THE BEST FISHING HOLES AND OUTFIT ME WITH EVERYTHING I NEED.

LET IT RAIN

Let My words fall like rain on tender grass,
like gentle showers on young plants.

DEUTERONOMY 32:2 NLT

A rain shower starts as an occasional plunk on the windowpane. Soon, though, the sound shifts to a steady, dull roar not unlike the sound machine that lulls some to sleep each night. The dark clouds and gentle noise beckon you to curl up and listen for as long as your schedule will allow. It's the perfect moment for a little more rest and maybe some reading. Isn't that why God gave us rainy days? Maybe.

God gives us all kinds of invitations to slow down and rest—not necessarily to sleep every time, but to rest in Him and His presence. Just as plants grow hot and tired under the sun's heat, as beautiful and needed as those rays may be, so we too dry out and wilt when we fail to slow down and hydrate our souls. God is waiting to pour out His life-giving water into your day through the nourishing power of prayer and reading His Word. When we take a few moments to soak in His goodness, we are refreshed and empowered to handle the day's tasks in God's strength instead of our own. As we are properly nourished, God produces in us lasting fruit, the kind that blesses and strengthens those around us. Whether it's rainy or sunny outside your window, take a few minutes before the crazy pace of the day begins. Quiet your soul before God and let the truth of His love pour into and out of your life today.

LORD,
"I LIFT MY HANDS
TO YOU IN PRAYER.
I THIRST FOR YOU AS
PARCHED LAND
THIRSTS FOR RAIN"
(PSALM 143:6 NLT).

WORRY-FREE LIVING

Don't worry about anything;

instead, pray about everything.

PHILIPPIANS 4:6 NLT

You just can't help worrying! And there's no lack of things to worry about, is there? God knows the thoughts that keep coming at you, the worries that whirl around in your head all day, and the anxiety that keeps you up at night. They are strong, pervasive, and persistent. But God isn't giving you a pat on the head when He says, "Don't worry." Instead, He teaches you how not to worry.

First, God urges you to pray about everything that agonizes you—big or small. If it's a concern to you, it's a concern to Him. He wants you to pull it right out of your head and give it to Him and then leave it with Him! Second, He invites you to remember all the things you've worried about in the past that didn't happen. He was taking care of you then just as He is now and will in the future. Third, He asks you to trust and rely on Him because He cares about you, and that's not going to change.

When God says, "Don't worry," take Him at His Word. Allow yourself the joy and peace of a worry-free day—and night.

DEAR GOD, FREE ME FROM THE HABIT OF CONSTANT WORRY. WHEN WORRIES THREATEN ME, REMIND ME THAT YOU ARE THERE FOR ME TO TRUST AND RELY ON. GRANT ME THE PEACE OF HEART AND MIND THAT I CAN ONLY FIND IN YOU. AMEN.

A TIME TO SIT AND THINK

Relax, everything's going to be all right; rest, everything's coming together; open your hearts, love is on the way!

JUDE 1:1-2 THE MESSAGE

God's best is always grounded in love, and it's always what He wants for our lives: the best next step; the best path to our growth; the best outcome. We all have days when the waves crash relentlessly. Those don't feel the best. They are the days when the deeper breaths are needed, the fearless faith is tested, and blind trust that everything comes together for our good is more important than the overwhelming circumstances in front of us. Especially when it seems as if circumstances have washed away all our hopes and dreams.

Our days come one at a time, and the grace sufficient to handle each 24-hour increment comes, too, without fail. We have what we need when we need it. Not every day will be a day at the beach, physically or spiritually. But every day will move us toward a place where we exercise more trust, enjoy more peace, and look a little more like Jesus. All that really matters is what we do to point others to Him. Some things we pack in our day-to-day "survival" bags weigh us down and slow our progress. God allows the washing away of the dependencies we hold too tightly, the self-security we lean on too heavily, and the material things distracting us way too often. He wants us to rest in Him like we relax on a day at the beach. A time to sit and think about the magnitude of His love and the never-ending waves of His grace is a day worth planning.

FATHER, I'M RELAXED IN YOUR LOVING CARE TODAY. I TRUST EVERYTHING'S COMING TOGETHER FOR MY GOOD—WITH AN OCEAN OF LOVE BEHIND IT.

Relax,
EVERYTHING'S
GOING TO BE ALL RIGHT;
REST, EVERYTHING'S
COMING TOGETHER;
OPEN YOUR
HEARTS,
love is
on the way!

JUDE 1:1-2 THE MESSAGE

LET'S HEAR IT FOR KUDZU!

And the LORD God arranged for a leafy plant to grow there, and soon it spread its broad leaves over Jonah's head, shading him from the sun. This eased his discomfort, and Jonah was very grateful for the plant.

JONAH 4:6 NLT

Kudzu is a climbing, coiling, perennial vine with a capacity for acclerated growth that is virtually unstoppable. Late in the nineteenth century, America's most infamous weed was introduced from Asia to the highways and byways of this country as a garden plant and a boon to agriculture. The invasive plant seems to grow a mile a minute, eating up millions of acres of native plants and creating other-worldly landscapes of tangled, eerie looking shapes.

But the truth is, kudzu may not be all that bad. During times of drought, bees forage on kudzu nectar from the plant's grape-scented blossoms and produce a unique red- or purple-hued honey that tastes like grape jelly or bubblegum. The plant can also be utilized as a food ingredient or for animal feed, basketry, clothing, medicine, toiletries, compost, and the production of ethanol.

The plant God prepared for Jonah that would ease his discomfort in the heat of the fierce sun grew up overnight. God created that much-appreciated plant, and He created kudzu as well. Sometimes what we see as "bad" may actually be a benefit and a blessing to humanity.

> FATHER, HELP ME SEE THE GOOD IN THINGS THAT SEEM INVASIVELY BAD. BEAUTY DOES NOT REPRESENT PURITY, AND INVASIVE SPECIES DON'T ALWAYS NEED TO BE REMOVED. HELP ME GIVE THANKS FOR GOOD FROM WHEREVER IT COMES.

GARDEN GROWTH

The seed that fell on good soil represents those who truly hear and understand God's Word and produce a harvest of thirty, sixty, or even a hundred times as much as had been planted!

MATTHEW 13:23 NLT

Imagine being led through a home until you reach the back door, where you are encouraged to walk into the garden. As you push open the door, your eyes take in the beautiful scene spreading before you, the most spectacular garden you have ever seen. A graceful weeping willow guards the corner, dozens of daffodils stand at attention, and brilliant pink and red peonies, encore azaleas, and a variety of ferns and tall grasses line a pebbled pathway. The owner must be proud of this handiwork. "What's your secret?" you ask. Smiling, they answer, "The secret's in the soil."

Before we ever plant a single bulb, the soil must be tilled. Sometimes it requires additional nutrients to make the conditions ripe for planting. But rooted in the right soil, beautiful growth is inevitable.

Our hearts are much like our gardens. We may all hear the message of truth about God's grace and forgiveness, but only hearts that are tilled with humility and repentance are seasoned properly to receive those spiritual seeds. When we are open to receive God's grace, acknowledging our desperate need for Him, the light of His Son streams down, the richness of truth feeds us, and our lives sprout into a beautiful display of His magnificent handiwork. This morning, ask God to tend to the soil of your soul. Then experience the beautiful growth God brings to your life.

LORD, PLEASE PLANT ME IN GOOD SOIL AND SEND PLENTY OF WATER SO THAT I MAY GROW INTO A SPLENDID VINE AND PRODUCE RICH SPIRITUAL FRUIT.

SEEING GOD'S HAND IN A DIFFERENT WAY

I am holding you by your right hand...don't be afraid;

I am here to help you.

ISAIAH 41:13 TLB

Have you noticed all the hand-holding in public places? Elderly couples offer each other support. Dads and moms keep their little ones safe. Young couples express their budding romance. Good friends make good memories. Holding hands is a heartwarming gesture that keeps us feeling connected, safe, and loved while on life's journey. We're not wired to walk it alone and, because we belong to God, we never have to. When God says He's holding us by our right hand, it means He's present in our need right now.

The loving Father that He is, He encourages us further with "Don't be afraid." To reiterate, He's got us by the hand and He's not going anywhere. How can we feel held by a Father we can't physically see or touch? What if we started seeing Him in other ways? The next time you spot the beauty of a butterfly in flight, remember, God is going to do a brand-new thing. See, He's already begun (Isaiah 43:19)—or when sparrows come to and from your bird feeder, be reminded, "Not one sparrow...can fall to the ground without your Father knowing it" (Matthew 10:29 TLB).

His Word comes to life all around us. We merely have to sharpen our spiritual eyesight and keep our mind and heart looking up to see it. When we are filled with the Father's promises, lies get crowded out completely, lies like, "No one cares about you"; "You're all alone in this world"; or "You have nothing to put your hope in." The rejoicing of our heart is knowing that not one of these is true.

FATHER, SHOW ME WHAT YOU WANT ME TO SEE. THANK YOU THAT NO MATTER HOW I FEEL, I'M NEVER ALONE.

A HOPE THAT GROWS

I rejoice and am glad.

Even my body has hope.

PSALM 16:9 NCV

You could say that hope is like a life preserver in the midst of a storm at sea. Without it, one's head would slip below the waves of discouragement and despair. We don't just need hope. We won't survive without it.

Hope disappears when we depend too much on people and things that fail us and leave us stranded on an "island of hopeless." It's even risky to place our hope in our national pride or on concepts like the inherent goodness of humankind. Everybody and everything fails eventually—but not God. Place your hope in Him and you will never find yourself feeling hopeless again.

When storm clouds gather on the horizon or a torrential downpour of calamity catches you by surprise, hold fast to your hope in God. Read and meditate on His promises in the Bible. Then learn to trust Him with one situation at a time. Soon your heart will be filled with hope and the storm clouds will no longer signal doom. Instead they will represent opportunities to place your hope again and again in your great and loving God.

DEAR LORD, I'VE ALREADY DISCOVERED THAT THERE'S HOPE IN THIS WORLD FOR ME. SHOW ME THAT HOPE CAN GROW AND THRIVE IN MY HEART AS I PLACE ALL I HAVE IN YOUR MIGHTY HANDS. AMEN.

THE FORECAST FOR TODAY

Though your sins are like scarlet,
I will make them as white as snow.

ISAIAH 1:18 NLT

You heard the weather report, but you weren't sure it would pan out. It wouldn't be the first time you'd awakened in the morning hoping to find snow on the ground, only to see a soggy mess instead. But today was different. The light shining through the cracks in the blinds seemed brighter than before. So you tugged the shade's cord and pulled open the view to a brand-new world. All the dreary browns and grays of winter had vanished; in their place, pristine snow glistened against a brilliant blue sky. Nestled on tree branches, streets, cars, and everything in between, the weather miracle transformed the bleak world you'd known into a scene of magic, mystery, and undeniable beauty.

Better than any forecaster, God has issued a prediction for your day—no matter the physical weather outside your doors. If you are trusting Him to make the landscape of your life brighter than before, you will wake up each day discovering a truth better than transient snow: God wipes your slate perfectly clean each new morning. The failures and regrets of yesterday are completely covered by His love and forgiveness. You are free to enjoy the beauty of all He is as you discover the treasures He has hidden for you in this day.

Unlike the weather, God's miracle of grace never changes, never fades away. You are forever forgiven simply through faith in Him. Praise God for His mysterious, permanent, and undeniably beautiful gift of daily grace!

THANK YOU, LORD, FOR FORGIVENESS AND A BEAUTIFUL RELATIONSHIP WITH YOU. I ACKNOWLEDGE MY NEED FOR YOU AND RECEIVE YOUR FORGIVENESS. AMEN.

YOUR FAITH IS SHOWING

I planted the seed in your hearts...
but it was God who made it grow.

1 CORINTHIANS 3:6 NLT

Peel an orange and drop a seed into the ground. Given time, sunlight, and fertile soil, you will get an orange tree. Not an apple, pear, or lemon tree, but a tree that can do nothing other than produce—surprise, surprise—oranges.

God's Spirit has planted the seed of faith in your heart. Now He is moistening it with the living water of God's Word, warming it with His protection and care, and nurturing it with His presence. Given time, is it any surprise that you will start bearing the fruit of faith—goodness, kindness, patience, peace? If that orange seed you planted developed into a strong healthy tree and produced more good oranges every season, you'd be pleased but not astonished. The same is true with you. The increasingly abundant fruit of your faith is what God has been expecting all along! Let the good seed that God has planted in you grow deep-rooted and strong. Don't worry about what kind of fruit will grow—that's already been established by the One who planted the seed!

THANK YOU, FATHER, FOR PLANTING GOOD SEED IN ME. I WANT TO SEE THAT SEED GROW AND PRODUCE FRUIT. PLEASE GUIDE ME AND FEED ME SO I BEAR FRUITS OF FAITH.

GENUINE HAPPINESS

Let love be genuine.

ROMANS 12:9 ESV

God had compassion for the people of Nineveh (a great city full of wicked people who were serving false gods). He asked Jonah to go to Nineveh and let the people know that if they didn't stop their ways, they would all be destroyed. However, Jonah didn't want to warn the people. He didn't think they deserved to be saved, so he disobeyed and took a boat to Tarshish and eventually found himself in the belly of a whale. Jonah was a disobedient prophet who did not want to set his mind on things above. He was quick to judge others while neglecting to examine his own heart. God's love for Nineveh resulted in the repentance of 120,000 people, but Jonah was too fixated on his own life to experience genuine happiness for them. God cared about the people, but Jonah cared about himself.

Have you ever been in Jonah's shoes, unable to experience genuine happiness for others because you yourself were in the way? We have all been there for reasons we wouldn't care to admit, such as pride, jealousy, comparison, or self-pity. But genuine happiness calls us to think beyond ourselves and invite God into the process of changing our heart. Genuine happiness comes from a place of pure love. Are you genuinely happy when others succeed, or is Jonah's story too close to home?

LORD, I WANT TO REJOICE WITH OTHERS WHEN THEY REJOICE. HELP ME GET OVER MYSELF SO THAT I CAN FULLY, GENUINELY BE HAPPY WHEN GOOD THINGS HAPPEN FOR OTHERS, EVEN WHEN GOOD THINGS AREN'T HAPPENING FOR ME.

STAR OF WONDER

God saw that the light was good.
Then He separated the light from the darkness.

GENESIS 1:4 NLT

Have you ever wondered what it's like where the stars live? Not the celebrity kind of stars, but the celestial sort—those curious, gleaming beams of light we see shining through the darkness of night. Can you imagine getting closer? The brightness and burning would be so intense that we couldn't describe it. A ball of surging power, radiating glory as it sits alone, suspended in space. Though deepest darkness lies all around, its light shines greater, sending energy in waves countless light-years away.

What a miracle each star is! What a wonder that God would compare us to each of these, yet He did. When we look up at the night sky, we witness God's picture of His people, their lives filled with the glory of His incredible power and brilliance. Burning with a supernatural passion for real beauty and truth, we stand out in the darkness of this world. And for some who come near, our fire is too bright, too intense for them. With no light of their own, the lost often prefer the darkness. But don't be discouraged. Starlight also illuminates our world and lights the way for those who recognize their need. Today, fuel up on the power of God's Word. Invite His presence inside you to chase away any shadows of self-doubt and let His love illuminate the world with wonderful light through you.

DEAR HEAVENLY FATHER, HELP ME TO STAND OUT IN THE DARKNESS AS A STAR OF YOUR LIGHT. USE ME TO ILLUMINATE BEAUTY AND TRUTH. DRAW THOSE IN DARKNESS TO YOUR WONDERFUL LIGHT.

SHIFTING OUR LOAD

Yes, my soul, find rest in God;

my hope comes from Him.

PSALM 62:5 NIV

Rest can feel like an impossible thing to accomplish in our everyday lives. There's always so much to keep us on the run. There are too many lists to look at, to-dos to get done, and demands to attend to. Our bodies need rest to be restored and energized, but our spirits need rest to keep our bodies well. That's why God encourages us to rest and give Him every care, even the ones we've gotten in the habit of picking up again and again.

Not only does the "picking up" weigh us down, but it holds us back from the beautiful freedom Jesus provided. He sacrificed everything so that, through grace, all the heavy lifting is done for us. When we take His way and His will, we don't get worn out. We can leave fear at His feet with the confidence: "God has not given us a spirit of fear and timidity, but of power, love, and self-discipline" (II Timothy 1:7 NLT). We can leave self-doubt and insecurity beneath the certainty: "With God, everything is possible" (Matthew 19:26 TLB). There will always be enough. He will always be our courage. We are going to see the desires He placed in our hearts come to pass. Giving our spirit the rest it requires will give our mind the break it needs to face the day with the hope. If we let God lighten our mental load today, we'll have room for His love to flow through us even more.

FATHER, I GIVE YOU MY CARES AND ALL THE MENTAL CLUTTER THAT KEEPS ME FROM LOVING AND SERVING YOU COMPLETELY—SPIRIT, SOUL, AND BODY. HELP ME SEE THE NEEDS AROUND ME BY TRUSTING ALL OF MINE TO YOU.

COME AGAIN ANOTHER DAY

The LORD God had not caused it to rain.

GENESIS 2:5 KJV

Can you imagine living in a world without rain? There were no weather forecasters or rained-out picnics in Noah's day. The Bible says that Noah had never seen rain, much less torrential rain or destructive floods of water. Before the Great Flood, streams and rivers watered the plants as well as springs of water that flowed upward from under the earth to mist and hydrate the plants. So Noah had to take God's word in faith for this thing called "rain" and follow God's instructions to prepare for a dystopian event he could never even imagine (Genesis 6:5). "By faith Noah, being warned by God concerning events as yet unseen, in reverent fear constructed an ark for the saving of his household" (Hebrews 11:7 ESV). And God saved Noah and his family along with a menagerie of animals inside that huge ark constructed of wood.

God made a covenant promise to us that He would never again destroy the earth with a flood. He sealed this promise with a bow of colors in the sky that could only appear with the presence of instability in the atmosphere known as rain. "I do set My bow in the cloud, and it shall be for a token of a covenant between Me and the earth (Genesis 9:13 KJV). When there is instability in the atmosphere of your life, remember that we are living arks for God to dwell in, holding the promise of eternal life with Him, that those who believe will not perish.

THANK YOU, LORD, FOR RAINBOWS. THANK YOU THAT THEY REPRESENT YOUR FAITHFULNESS IN THE STORMS OF LIFE. LORD, HELP ME TO HAVE FAITH THAT A RAINBOW WILL COME EVEN WHEN I CAN'T UNDERSTAND THE INSTABILITY THAT IS CAUSING THE RAIN. I TRUST IN YOU.

THE ABUNDANCE OF LITTLE

Many are called, but few are chosen.

MATTHEW 22:14 ESV

When we want something, we tend to think of bigger as better. More rather than less. We want a bigger house. Lots of money. Larger portions of food. We want our lives to overflow with an overabundance of everything.

Israel was impressed with Saul because he was a tall drink of water. But God looks at the heart, and King Saul's heart was not right before God. In God's economy, little is much. He can take a shepherd boy and transform him into King David (I Samuel 16:13). He can save a widow and her family from starvation with an ever-flowing cruet of oil (II Kings 4:2). Jesus can take a little boy's lunch of a few loaves and fishes and feed thousands with leftovers to spare (John 6:1–14). God can raise up a farmer like Gideon to lead a ragtag army of a few hundred men against thousands of soldiers and prevail against them (Judges 7:1–7). "Five of you will chase a hundred, and a hundred of you will chase ten thousand, and your enemies will fall by the sword before you" (Leviticus 26:8 NIV). Over and over in Scripture, God chooses the lowly, the underdog, the youngest and most inexperienced, and the least likely to succeed based on human assessment. And inexplicably, from the least of us, He brings forth much.

HEAVENLY FATHER, THANK YOU FOR SEEING THE VALUE IN THE LITTLE I HAVE TO OFFER. FATHER, MAKE MY LITTLE MORE THAN ENOUGH. MULTIPLY MY TALENTS, GIFTS, AND BLESSINGS TO BLESS OTHERS IN ABUNDANCE.

ETERNITY ALL AROUND US!

God has made everything beautiful for its own time. He has planted eternity in the human heart, but even so, people cannot see the whole scope of God's work from beginning to end.

ECCLESIASTES 3:11 NLT

Brianna made her bed and then headed to the kitchen to make breakfast. But something made her go back to the bedroom window to have a peek. She hoped to see a bunny hiding in the grass or a deer munching nearby. Nothing. She stepped away, but once again she felt compelled to go back to the window. Thinking it might be God prompting her, she took a deeper, closer look. Still nothing. Just the usual, the ordinary—a ravine embraced by trees, grass, and a dead stump. Brianna asked the Lord, "Is that You, Lord?" Then just as she was feeling a bit silly, the Lord said to Brianna in her spirit, "Look. Don't you see it? Eternity is all around you. Now." She gasped at the words. Brianna would never see life on this earth the same again.

God had planted eternity in her heart, a divine sense of purpose and a mysterious yearning that nothing would be able to satisfy but God Himself. Just like Brianna, we can live with that beautiful knowledge not merely when we are in heaven, but right now. Yes, these ordained moments—one after the other, as if threaded together into a priceless string of pearls—are anything but usual or ordinary! They are pearls of eternity.

LORD, THANK YOU FOR GIVING ME THE HOPE OF ETERNITY WITH YOU. I SEE IT ALL AROUND ME— IN NATURE, IN THE FACE OF NEWBORNS, IN COMPASSION.... HELP ME NEVER TO TAKE THE ORDINARY, EVERYDAY THINGS FOR GRANTED. HELP ME SEE THEM FOR THE GIFT THEY ARE.

SUNRISE SURPRISE

As surely as the sun rises, He will appear; He will come to us like the winter rains, like the spring rains that water the earth.

HOSEA 6:3 NIV

When it is still, quiet, and dark outside, during the wee hours of a cool summer morning, if you find a favorite outdoor spot and wait, you can witness the glory of morning. Slowly, as eyes adjust to the darkness, the trees and shrubs seem to be whitewashed silhouettes in a lonely, gray world. Then it happens. The first rays of light peek over the horizon. Sky and hills and branches and blades of grass catch the energy, and color pours onto every lighted surface. Like magic, light dispels the darkness and animals respond on cue, chattering and chirping to greet the morning. As pink and orange hues paint the pale blue sky, it is the perfect time and place to soak up the beauty, the miracle of the morning's sunrise. It makes the heart want to join in their song and sets the mind on things above.

If you rise early enough each day, you can witness this blessing again and again. Daily, God brings our earth around for the sun to shine on our lives, initiating beauty from the very beginning. It begs us to begin our day mindful of the Master Painter, Sustainer, and Source of all we call beautiful. He is with you in all those sacred moments where light chases away the darkness. He reminds us day after day that His goodness rises to greet us and the sweetness of His morning touch lingers for the rest of our day.

CREATOR OF THE UNIVERSE, THANK YOU FOR EACH NEW DAY. THANK YOU FOR THE BIRDSONG, THE SOFT BREEZES, AND THE BEAUTY OF A SUNRISE. LORD, HELP ME REMEMBER EVERY MORNING TO PRAISE YOU AS THE MASTER PAINTER, SUSTAINER, AND SOURCE OF ALL.

BREATHE IN

Praise Him under the open skies;

praise Him for His acts of power,

praise Him for His magnificent greatness.

PSALM 150:1–2 THE MESSAGE

Have you ever ridden a bicycle on the beach early in the morning? You get to see a lot more of the shoreline than you would on a walk, and the salty air comes at you faster, filling your lungs with the freshness of it all. It's like getting a big gulp of God's goodness surrounded by the magnificent greatness of His creation. It so refreshing!

Spending time outdoors can set off a chorus of internal praise. It sometimes feels as if the heart is actually swelling from seeing the beauty of it. Before you know it, you're overwhelmed with gratitude. To think, He made all this because He loves us and wants us to feel that way. He designed the earth to encourage our hearts to look up to Him and connect with His creation—starry skies, pink sunsets, and aqua-blue waters all reflect His eternal power. If we're having a down day, nature is a good place to get a pick-me-up.

Our hearts aren't getting much of a break these days. So many things in the world are changing so rapidly that it's hard to keep up. But God is the same yesterday, today, and forever. His infallible, unchanging Word is the one thing we can hold onto for the hope we need. It's a good time to get outside and be reminded that every part of this created earth is a love song written to us by our Father.

FATHER, THANK YOU FOR THE BEAUTY OF CREATION AND THE POWER OF YOUR PRESENCE IN IT. HELP ME BREATHE IT IN EVERY DAY.

THE PERFECT PLACE

Rejoice in the Lord always. I will say it again: Rejoice! Let your gentleness be evident to all. The Lord is near. Do not be anxious about anything, but in every situation, by prayer and petition, with thanksgiving, present your requests to God. And the peace of God, which transcends all understanding, will guard your hearts and your minds in Christ Jesus.

PHILIPPIANS 4:4–7 NIV

*I*t was late afternoon and she had a little time on her hands before dinner. Sitting at her computer, she started to surf. Pictures and messages reminded her of people she hadn't seen in years, and before she knew it, she was scrolling through photo after perfect photo, looking at the fun and fellowship everyone else seemed to be having. Even as she clicked "Like," she couldn't help wanting . . . wishing . . . wondering if her life would ever be that good.

Then she went outside. The sun was setting behind the trees, brilliant streaks of pink and gold gilding a faint blue sky. A light breeze blew as the cicadas stirred in evening celebration. She sank onto a chair to enjoy the show, God's glory cast through chorus and color. In her pleasure, she felt God's presence. In His nearness, she gave thanks, her gratitude for God's goodness washing away the discontent.

In giving thanks, we find our rightful place in this world and rest for our searching souls. We are the recipients of God's extraordinary grace, the object of His undeserved favor. In the moments of our lives—the fun and the fearful ones and the successes and the failures—we live loved. All of eternity, beginning before our birth, has been purchased for us at the highest price, our future secured by our loving Savior. The beauty of creation sings with worship and wonder at such extravagant love lavished on us, God's beloved children. Let us join in with song!

FATHER, SHOW ME ALL THE WAYS I CAN PRAISE YOU TODAY. OPEN MY EYES TO EVERY OPPORTUNITY TO SHOW GRATITUDE AND LOVE. AMEN.

WAYMAKER

Strengthen the feeble hands, steady the knees that give way;
say to those with fearful hearts, "Be strong, do not fear; your God will come...."
Water will gush forth in the wilderness and streams in the desert.
The burning sand will become a pool, the thirsty ground bubbling springs....
And a highway will be there; it will be called the Way of Holiness;
it will be for those who walk on that Way.

ISAIAH 35:3–4, 6–8 NIV

For years she and her husband had been at odds, their personality traits that once drew them together now driving them apart. Between work and the kids, they barely had any time together. Whenever they tried, bitterness surfaced. Separation seemed the only answer, despair waiting around the corner.

They felt trapped—not unlike God's people so many years ago. The Israelites had left their homes in Egypt in hopes of finding a better life together—with God. But not long into the journey, their path ended at the Red Sea. Or so it seemed. Enemies pursued them and certain doom awaited.

But God had a plan all along, positioning them for a miracle. As they cried out, God parted the waves. His people walked through safely while their enemies were crushed. God has a flawless history of making a way when all hope is gone. Just look to the cross: even the darkest hours gave way to a new and lasting dawn in His presence. God's power raises the dead to life and opens doors we thought were locked forever.

What Red Sea roadblock are you facing today? Will you wilt in fear or turn your focus to your waymaking God? Don't let your enemy convince you that all hope is lost. Every relationship and each situation in life serves to help us see God in a new light. Let your worries lead you to the God who saves and He will light your way.

JESUS, THANK YOU FOR MAKING A WAY FOR ME. HELP ME TO NEVER LOSE SIGHT OF YOUR LOVE, COMFORT, AND POWER TO RESTORE AND RENEW. I LOVE YOU.

SIGNS OF SPRING

Behold, I will do a new thing; now it shall spring forth; shall ye not know it? I will even make a way in the wilderness, and rivers in the desert.

ISAIAH 43:19 KJV

*I*n spring, buds burst out on tree branches, the grass gets greener, and days become warmer. Fragrant, colorful flowers fill in the landscape, followed by larger, spectacular displays of the trees and shrubs. Birds and crickets and frogs and cicadas come out of hiding and call for spring to come in full.

While the snow and stark vestiges of winter have a beauty and charm of their own, there's something special about spring and the new hope it brings. The world is just a bit brighter and our breathing lighter—as if, with the change of weather, the weight of the world has lifted a little. In all seasons the signs and hope of spring is alive even if buried deep beneath the surface.

God's goodness grows in you and your life's circumstances in much the same way. Though situations may seem bleak during certain seasons of your life, God's love and purpose never lie dormant. He is affecting the greatest transformation you can imagine, setting the stage for your growth to bloom for His glory. If you find yourself in a season of waiting, then set your eyes on God and settle in for the upcoming show. In His time, you'll see the telltale signs of spring. It's then that we will celebrate the growth only God can bring.

FATHER, THANK YOU FOR GROWTH THAT BURSTS FORTH AT JUST THE RIGHT TIME. HELP ME TO STAY FAITHFUL IN THE DORMANT SEASONS TO CELEBRATE THE GROWTH THAT IS TO COME.

ROOTS

Let your roots grow down into Him and draw up nourishment from Him.
See that you go on growing in the Lord,
and become strong and vigorous in the truth you were taught.
Let your lives overflow with joy and thanksgiving for all he has done.

COLOSSIANS 2:7 TLB

There's the intruder, sticking up right in the middle of the garden bed. You walk over and bend to pull up the errant oak tree seedling that has sprouted in the tulips. But the short seedling seems to have hidden strength. Wedging the weight of your body against the tree's resistance, slowly you feel its root system give way. With a tearing sound, the roots break and release their grip, long tendrils of underground anchorage slipping to the surface. Once fully uprooted, the small seedling is several feet in length. How could so much be happening underground with so little to show up top?

It's funny how small things can have that kind of impact on us. A little negative comment here or a white lie there can suddenly take root. Left unchecked, bitterness and apathy spread tenaciously, burrowing into our heart and mind, choking out the love and life that once dominated. On the surface others may only see small discontent. But inside, anger has taken hold with a viselike grip. To uproot it requires the full weight of your entire person, leaning in the opposite direction, with reliance upon God's great mercy. Then the seeds of God's love and forgiveness are freed to grow and bear the kind of fruit you want to see in your life.

Why not ask God to uproot any bitterness, complacency, or dishonesty lurking in your soul? Ask Him to plant a harvest of love, joy, and peace.

FATHER, I TRUST YOUR STRENGTH, YOUR PLANS FOR ME, AND YOUR LOVE. HELP ME LET GO OF EVERYTHING THAT IS HOLDING ME BACK FROM LIVING A PEACEFUL LIFE WITH YOU.

MAY YOUR ROOTS

go down deep

INTO THE SOIL

OF GOD'S

MARVELOUS

LOVE.

EPHESIANS 3:17 TLB

THE COMPANY TO KEEP

Keep company with Me and you'll learn to live freely and lightly.

MATTHEW 11:30 THE MESSAGE

What an invitation we get in Matthew 11:30! We can live freely and lightly without being confined by fear or weighed down by the cares of this world. How do we learn to live with such fearless freedom? By hanging out with God! Our time with Him can be as casual as having coffee with a friend or walking on a trail. And it will feel that comfortable when we do it often and know Him well. Do you have a set time every day when you pray, praise, give thanks, ask questions, seek answers, and soak in His beautiful, refreshing presence? How would your life change if you woke up each morning to a conversation with God? What would it be like to develop the habit of connecting with God all day long? Of course, there are times when it's necessary to get away from all distractions to pray and listen, but we also gain much by His continual counsel. Being mindful of His presence brings comfort.

"Rejoice always, pray continually, give thanks in all circumstances" (I Thessalonians 5:16–18 NIV) sounds like another invitation to keep company with God. It means staying tuned in and aware that He always looks forward to spending time with us. And He's always listening. Getting in the habit of continually praying teaches us, grows us, and rewards us with the joy of living freely and lightly. And divine joy is our strength. Strength to face fears. Strength to encourage others. Strength to manage emotions. Strength to be brave, forgive, and love. Strength to be more like Him.

FATHER, KEEPING COMPANY WITH YOU KEEPS ME JOYFUL AND STRONG. THANK YOU FOR ALWAYS BEING THERE.

CALMING THE STORM

He quiets the raging oceans
and all the world's clamor.

PSALM 65:7 TLB

There will be noisy days—not in sound, but in our mind. The list of things we need to do, the immediate things clamoring for our attention, the feeling of uncertainty about what's ahead. Our thought life feels like a raging ocean or a growling bear at times. How do we quiet it? How do we create enough calm to hear and know God's wisdom and direction? We trust that if He can quiet a raging ocean and a perilous storm by speaking to them, His words can also quiet our mind. "Lord, when doubts fill my mind, when my heart is in turmoil, quiet me and give me renewed hope and cheer" (Psalm 94:19 TLB).

We have the words. We have the choice to use them. And God has the power to back them! Every time the noise of this world tries to drown out the words He's given us, we have to mentally grab hold of them again—as many times a day as needed and as often as the doubts come. His words are the only thing that can truly quiet the mind. They're the life preserver that's always within reach. Even when we break down and our day feels unmanageable, our goals seem unreachable, and life feels unbearably out of control, the right words can give us strength to stand and keep standing. Once we speak truth and remind ourselves again that God can be trusted, we get braver in the face of our storms. They will not overtake us, because God cannot fail.

FATHER, THANK YOU FOR GIVING ME THE WORDS TO QUIET MY MIND AND KEEP MY SPIRIT CALM AND CONFIDENT IN YOU.

INTERMISSION

They that wait upon the LORD shall renew their strength.

ISAIAH 40:31 KJV

Warm breezes chased thin white clouds across an azure sky. Golden dandelions danced in the sun as the wind rustled through the tall green grass. *What a perfect day it's been*, you muse, seated on a hill overlooking the valley not far from your campsite. As you sit and watch the world around you, colors shift to deeper hues. On the horizon the sun sinks low, painting clouds with deep pinks and oranges as the shadows stretch long on the earth beneath. Even in the changing, the ending, you see an unsung beauty. The world has entered an intermission, the brilliance of day demanding a break until dawn. There is both a sadness and a satisfaction in the day that has been and anticipation for what's yet to come.

Sunsets color more than the skies. They fire our imagination and fill our soul with hope for a beauty that lasts beyond the day. They beckon us to be still, to embrace the necessity of endings to prepare for new beginnings. As much as we resist change and the uncertainty it brings, we see God painting promises for tomorrow every time the sun sets. In His hands, endings are only the temporary pause allowing us rest before even better blessings begin.

Are you nearing a season of change? Cast your cares on the One who commands the night and ushers in the dawn. Rest in the quiet, and trust God to shine the light on His purpose and plan for you when the time is right.

FATHER, IT'S SUCH A COMFORT KNOWING THAT, EVEN WHEN IT SEEMS AS IF EVERYTHING AROUND ME IS CHANGING, YOU ARE CONSTANT AND FOREVER AND YOU WILL NEVER LET ME GO.

MADE BY HAND

He created them male and female,

and He blessed them.

GENESIS 5:2 NASB

We enjoy receiving gifts that have been thoughtfully chosen and graciously given. But what about gifts that are thoughtfully chosen, graciously given, and lovingly made by hand? Those gifts often mean the most because we know that the giver spent more than money. They spent their time, talents, and effort to create a one-of-a-kind gift just for us.

Have you ever seen yourself as God's one-of-a-kind gift? His unique handiwork? His blessing to those around you? Wherever you go, you're bringing your personal perspective, individual abilities, and distinctive presence—and not by chance, because God is not one to waste the work of His hands. Perhaps your caring helps a loved one cope or a friend survive a tough time. Maybe your understanding calms a troubled heart or your smile lifts a sagging mood. Then again, it could be a past experience of yours that gives you the knowledge that allows you to help where no one else can!

You have been lovingly made by God's hand. He has thoughtfully chosen you, and He has graciously given you your life for a purpose. Wherever you go today, know that no one but one-of-a-kind you will do!

DEAREST FATHER, THANK YOU FOR GIVING ME UNIQUE GIFTS AND ABILITIES. HELP ME TO USE MY TALENTS TO CONNECT WITH OTHERS AT THE HEART LEVEL.

A SONG TO SING

I will sing to the LORD as long as I live.
I will praise my God to my last breath!

PSALM 104:33 NLT

Have you ever awakened to the sound of a solitary bird singing in the breaking dawn? Have you lingered at the window, letting the cheery chirps from that single warbler charm you? The little songsters sing wherever they happen to be, perhaps for no other reason than that they have a song to sing!

You don't need to have a special reason to talk to God. There's no need to plan your words or prepare a formal speech or recite a time-honored prayer before God will bend His ear to you. Why wait until you're in a bind to immerse yourself in the joy of His presence? Sometimes the most beautiful song is the one sung from an ordinary branch, on an ordinary tree, in an ordinary place, on an ordinary day, just for the pleasure of singing. God is everywhere! Everywhere you live and work, exercise and play. He's open to your spontaneous prayers and extemporaneous bursts of thanksgiving when the thought pops into your mind. When you want to sing, He's delighted to hear the sound of your voice!

LORD, I LOVE YOU.
I PRAISE YOU.
IN THE ORDINARINESS OF
TODAY I WANT TO SING
BECAUSE YOU HAVE GIVEN
ME A VOICE, BECAUSE I
HAVE BREATH, BECAUSE
I WANT MY WORDS
TO DEMONSTRATE MY
GRATITUDE. I WILL SING
FOR AS LONG AS I LIVE.

THE HOMECOMING

"This my son was dead, and is alive again;
he was lost, and is found."
And they began to celebrate.

LUKE 15:24 ESV

Most of us know the story of the prodigal son. He got the bright idea of asking his father to give him his inheritance early so he could journey to a far country and party hearty. But the gravity of the request escaped him. Asking for an early inheritance was an extreme insult, like telling his dad he wished he were dead. Though the father's heart was wounded to the core, he gave his son what he asked. And the son pursued a path of reckless living until he was so poor that he couldn't jump over a nickel to save a dime. He was so hungry that the carob pods he was feeding the pigs started to look good. So the prodigal son decided to return home even if he had to work as a servant in his father's house.

Meanwhile, back at the ranch, his loving father kept praying for his son to return home. And when he spotted the tiny speck of his son in the distance, he ran and embraced him. He was so overjoyed to have his son back that he called for the servants to bring the best robe for his son to wear, to put shoes on his feet and a ring on his hand, and to prepare a feast to celebrate his son's return. The prodigal's father is a wonderful example of how our loving Father receives us when we repent and "come home." Can we do less with people who have wounded or disappointed us? Salvation is truly cause for celebration.

FATHER, THANK YOU FOR WELCOMING ME HOME WHENEVER I HAVE WONDERED AWAY. LORD, HELP ME TO ALWAYS FIND MY WAY HOME.

HOPE SINGS

Why am I discouraged? Why is my heart so sad? I will put my hope in God! I will praise Him again—my Savior and my God! Now I am deeply discouraged, but I will remember you—even from distant Mount Hermon, the source of the Jordan, from the land of Mount Mizar. I hear the tumult of the raging seas as your waves and surging tides sweep over me. But each day the LORD pours His unfailing love upon me, and through each night I sing His songs, praying to God who gives me life.

PSALM 42:5–8 NLT

As she swept the floor (for the umpteenth this week), her mind wandered. Sometimes she felt angry, seeing all the junk left on the counters and floors, her family failing to notice the toll their negligence took. But then she saw an old toy tucked into a corner and it warmed her heart.

Like a mental seesaw, her emotions rose and fell depending on her focus, both positive and negative fighting for the high seat. The fight in her head sapped more strength than the sweeping! Even in solitude, she needed some peace! She turned on some praise music, and that move made all the difference.

We know by experience that music moves us in ways nothing else can. But music that lifts our Lord's name in praise does even more, taking our thoughts to a new level and transforming our mind to make them like His. As we listen to truth and agree in song, our souls are soothed by God's all-encompassing goodness. God's greatness brings light to our darkness. In His presence, our mind changes and our soul is moved to work in sync with the Spirit. Praise is God's secret weapon that silences distraction and focuses our heart where it belongs—at home with our Lord.

THANK YOU, GOD, FOR AWAKENING MY SOUL SO THAT I MAY LIVE PEACEFULLY AND JOYFULLY IN YOUR PRESENCE. AMEN.

THE AUTHOR

Every day of my life was recorded in your book.
Every moment was laid out before a single day had passed.

PSALM 139:16 NLT

You just wanted to buy an encouraging book for a friend and maybe pick up a good read for yourself while you were there. But the moment you opened the door to your favorite bookstore, your senses were overwhelmed by colors, titles, and topics. It seemed as if everyone in the world had written something and it was up to you to search until you found that one selection perfect for the occasion. Then you found yourself engrossed in book after book, the back-cover teasers leading you into the stories contained in those pages. Though there was a sea of options, each book had a different and captivating angle on life that broadened your thinking and piqued your interest. Each book was an unexpected adventure.

But adventure doesn't only happen in novels. It's happening in and through your life at this very moment. Today is not just another day. It's a pivotal page in the story that God is writing. Today is an integral part of the plot He's weaving to lead you closer to Himself and use you for purposes higher than you can imagine. He is inviting you to trust Him, because when you do—when you follow His prompts instead of trying to make the day fit your expectations—the plot thickens and the threads connect in unpredictable ways. Today, hand the pen to God and ask Him to write His story through your life. With Him in control, you'll know you've made the perfect selection.

YOU ARE THE AUTHOR OF MY LIFE, LORD. YOUR PLANS ARE SO MUCH BETTER THAN MINE. PLEASE HELP ME TRUST YOU WITH EACH CHAPTER AND GIVE CONTROL TO YOU.

TIME OF YOUR LIFE

Rest in the LORD and wait patiently for Him.

PSALM 37:7 NASB

If you want time to slow down, try watching the clock for fifteen minutes! With each passing second, the gap between them seems to stretch longer and longer, while you get more and more impatient. Five minutes later, you're ready to take the clock and throw it against the wall!

As you wait for God to unfold His plans for you, are you watching the clock? Say that nothing is happening that you believe shows His movement within you, much less what you would like to see take place around you. You get antsy! This is just taking too long! You think through your day-to-day experience and find no spiritual progress or demonstrable sign of His presence. So you watch the clock a few minutes more and then you give up. Does God have anything to do with your life at all?

DEAR GOD, I TRUST THAT YOU ARE WORKING ALL THINGS OUT FOR MY GOOD. HELP ME BE PATIENT AND REST IN THE KNOWLEDGE THAT YOU HAVE AMAZING PLANS FOR MY LIFE.

It's not easy to see sometimes, but God has everything to do with your life, your purpose, and your plans. Instead of "watching the clock," spend your time reflecting on His Word and appreciating what He has for you right now. Be patient. His time is always the right time.

MIRACLES ALL AROUND

Sing to Him; sing praises to Him.
Tell about all His miracles.

PSALM 105:2 NCV

While we long to see, hear, and feel miracles all around us, we rarely do. But life is full of miracles—great and small.

Imagine a curtain hanging between you and the outside world. Whatever lies on your side of the curtain—your daily routine, immediate responsibilities, and personal ambitions—gets your attention. From the time you get up in the morning until you tuck yourself into bed at night, it captures your full and complete concentration. No surprise: it's easy to forget that there's anything else out there, anything beyond your side of the curtain.

Consciously and deliberately set aside a few minutes each day to pull away all that separates you from the beauty, amazement, and heart-soaring joy of creation. As if for the first time, see flowers bending in the breeze, clouds floating across the sky, the face of a friend, your hand in the hand of another. Hear wind in the trees, rain on the roof, and the distant call of birds on the wing. Feel what it's like to hold a child, cuddle a pet, hug a loved one. Yes, the miracles of God's handiwork are all around us! Why not delight in them today?

FATHER, SHINE BRIGHTLY THROUGH MY LIFE TODAY, DRAWING MY EYES AND HEART TO THE BEAUTY OF YOUR MIRACLES AND THE WARMTH OF YOUR LOVE.

THE BEST OF CREATION

In the beginning
God created the heavens and the earth.

GENESIS 1:1 NASB

When God called the universe into being, our world was flawless. Imagine unspoiled earth and sky, land and seas, flowers and fields, mountains and valleys. What a breathtaking sight the world must have been, because God created everything absolutely perfectly, inside and out.

In our lives, we create things. We might establish a home for ourselves and our loved ones. Many among us build products or provide services to buyers, clients, and customers. Others form or join associations created to help and assist those in need. But are our creations perfect? Far from it, and we know that! But with God's original creation as our high standard, we also hold ourselves to high standards in whatever we do. God didn't scrimp or cheat or cut corners when He made the world for us, and that's why what we create—goods or services, physical things or intangible concepts—deserves nothing short of our best effort.

Name the most awe-inspiring nature scene you can think of. Look to a clear blue sky or a deep red rose. Let it remind you of the joy, pleasure, and privilege of your ability to create!

LORD, THANK YOU FOR CREATING A BEAUTIFUL WORLD FOR US TO LIVE IN! HELP ME USE MY CREATIVE ABILITIES TO HONOR YOU ALWAYS. AMEN.

MORNING SONG

Sing to the LORD a new song; sing to the LORD, all the earth.

PSALM 96:1 NASB

If you are still, you will see it. And if you listen, you can hear a symphony playing right outside your door. Don't bother looking for a bassoon or a clarinet, a cello or a trumpet. No man-made instruments are needed in God's performance hall. Instead, living creatures contribute their sound of praise to the Creator, with pitch and rhythm unique to their kind. Hummingbirds buzz from the summer lilacs, and tree frogs chirp from secret hiding places. Bullfrogs bellow in low, steady calls. Cicadas and crickets sound like maracas, and other birds are the woodwinds, their melodies sweetening the sound.

Are you delighted by the free concert outside your door day after day? God certainly is! He designed all His creatures to declare His praise in ways only they can. Something about music soothes our souls. It reminds us of a beauty greater, a power stronger, and a purpose eternal that exists beyond ourselves. Music in all its forms can lead us to worship when we remember the One who put the song in our heart in the first place. Perhaps that's why God chooses to live in the praises of His people. When we join in with all of creation, singing God's praise from grateful and thankful hearts, our lives join creation's symphony of praise and we are music to God's ears.

FATHER, MAKER OF THIS BEAUTIFUL WORLD, THANK YOU FOR THE GLORY OF NATURE. THANK YOU FOR USING IT TO COMFORT AND DELIGHT US. FATHER, HELP ME FIND COMFORT AND PEACE IN YOUR ARMS.

Whether you put on a praise CD, play worship music from your computer, or simply sing in your heart to God today, why not stand in awe of His beauty and love? Let His greatness inspire your heart and lips to declare His praise today.

CHEERFULLY EXPECTANT

Don't burn out; keep yourselves fueled and aflame. Be alert servants of the Master, cheerfully expectant. Don't quit in hard times; pray all the harder. Help needy Christians; be inventive in hospitality. Bless your enemies; no cursing under your breath. Laugh with your happy friends when they're happy; share tears when they're down. Get along with each other; don't be stuck-up. Make friends with nobodies; don't be the great somebody. Don't hit back; discover beauty in everyone. If you've got it in you, get along with everybody. Don't insist on getting even; that's not for you to do. "I'll do the judging," says God. "I'll take care of it."

ROMANS 12:11–19 THE MESSAGE

Scripture tells us to go buy your enemy lunch, if you see that they're hungry, or if they're thirsty, get them a drink. Your generosity will surprise them with goodness. Don't let evil get the best of you; get the best of evil by doing good. To be cheerfully expectant that God can do what we cannot within our own strength is in fact a *great* way to start each day, don't you think? God wants it all...not just in part.

Being cheerfully expectant means to have an expectant faith that knows God desires to do more than we would ever ask. The cheerfully expectant life is an intentional life of leaning into Jesus daily for the answers we need, both relationally and practically...with an expectant faith that He will work. God wants to show up, show off, and sell out in our lives. And when He shows up, there is no limit to what God can do!

LORD, I LIVE IN CHEERFUL EXPECTATION OF WHAT YOU WILL DO WITH MY LIFE. KEEP MY FAITH STRONG.

BOUNDARY OF LOVE

He's solid rock under my feet, breathing room for my soul.

PSALM 62:2 THE MESSAGE

Reaching a spot on a hiking trail where the landscape opens up to a breathtaking view is a stop-you-in-your-tracks moment. It's one that inspires everything in us to say "Thank God I'm alive!" It's a remarkable, memorable, and thoughtful experience. And it's incredibly good for our soul. God knew it would be; that's why He carved the hills and mountains so artistically. That's why He saturated nature with His beauty and love. And that's why we gain so much, physically and spiritually, by appreciating it.

God's attributes are far above our ability to describe them adequately, but without a doubt, love is the highest of them all. His love for us can't be pulled down by the weight of any wrongdoing, and it will never fall by way of unforgiveness. God's love for us isn't shaken by a single fear we have or any number of times we falter in our faith. His love for us can't be toppled by our refusal to listen, our running from His will, or our resisting the reality of it.

God's love for us is insurmountable and unstoppable. There's nothing more solid under our feet and nothing more refreshing to our soul. He's the "breathing room" we need to survive the sometimes-suffocating darkness in this world. Taking time to envelop ourselves in the things He made can prove to be the heavenly hug we need. Nature quiets the world and awakens our senses. It encourages us to see, hear, and praise Him. It opens our eyes to His all-encompassing love and His constant presence.

We can be thankful that His love for us is immovable and unmeasurable—and every breathtaking thing He made is proof of it.

DEAR GOD, THANK YOU FOR THE ART OF CREATION AND THE BEAUTY YOU PUT IN IT TO RESTORE OUR SOULS AND INSPIRE US TO SEE YOUR BOUNDLESS LOVE. YOU'RE SO GOOD!

ROOT OF THE MATTER

The earth causes plants to grow,

and a garden causes the seeds planted in it to grow.

In the same way the Lord GOD will make goodness

and praise come from all the nations.

ISAIAH 61:11 NCV

For every thriving flower garden, there's a busy gardener. Without their dedication, patience, effort, and know-how, weeds would quickly choke out lush blossoms. Without their willingness to prune and nurture prized plants and vines, healthy stalks would soon become weak and withered.

Your spiritual life and a flower garden share several things in common. First, they both need ongoing care and attention. Yes, God has planted seeds of faith in your heart, but He invites you to nurture them with daily Scripture reading, spiritual reflection, and heartfelt prayer. Second, negligence allows weeds such as materialism, addiction, and selfishness to suffocate the roots of faith. Once inner weeds get established, your relationship with God is easily overrun.

Third, a skillful gardener knows how to protect tender seedlings, prop up weak branches, dig out noxious growths, and prune blooming plants so that they yield bigger, brighter, and healthier blossoms. Your gardener is God. Ask Him to send His Spirit into the garden of your heart. Let Him get you to the root of a life resplendent with luscious, fragrant flowers to possess and give away!

FATHER, THANK YOU FOR BEING PATIENT, KIND, AND LOVING WITH ME AS I LEARN AND GROW IN MY SPIRITUAL WALK. PLEASE REMOVE THE THINGS IN MY LIFE THAT GET IN THE WAY OF MY RELATIONSHIP WITH YOU. AMEN.

HOW YOU SEE IT

God has made everything beautiful for its own time.

He has planted eternity in the human heart,

but even so, people cannot see the whole scope

of God's work from beginning to end.

ECCLESIASTES 3:11 NLT

Some of the latter paintings by famous Impressionist artist Claude Monet reflect the more vivid colors he was able to perceive after his cataract operation. He saw the world with one set of colors one day, and the next, he saw through a new color wheel that turned around his life and his art. We live in this world with extraordinary diversity in people, animals, plants, and colors, yet none of us are prepared for what we will see in heaven! We will marvel at vistas and landscapes we could never conceive of or imagine in our finite state. We will see new flowers and colors and live in the unfiltered light of God. Jesus has prepared a place for each believer and adorned it with His love.

First Corinthians 2:9 (KJV) says, "But as it is written, Eye hath not seen, nor ear heard, neither have entered into the heart of man, the things which God hath prepared for them that love Him." What we see now is a mere reflection in a dusty mirror, but one day we will see and understand all things clearly.

DEAR FATHER, THANK YOU FOR MAKING SUCH A BEAUTIFUL, DIVERSE WORLD. FATHER, OPEN MY EYES TO FULLY SEE THE BEAUTY AROUND ME, TO APPRECIATE THE COLORS, TEXTURES, AND SHAPES OF IT ALL. YOU ARE THE MASTER ARTIST.

THE UPSIDE OF UH-OH!

Live creatively, friends. If someone falls into sin, forgivingly restore him, saving your critical comments for yourself. You might be needing forgiveness before the day's out. Stoop down and reach out to those who are oppressed. Share their burdens, and so complete Christ's law. If you think you are too good for that, you are badly deceived.

GALATIANS 6:1–3 THE MESSAGE

A gracious host lets slip a tactless remark. A savvy company manager makes the worst possible business decision. A good friend fails to notice her best friend's need. No matter how capable and competent we are, we mess up sometimes!

Mistakes are embarrassing, and they bring us down a peg or two. But here's the upside. For starters, we're reminded that we're human just like everyone else. And then we're compelled to ask forgiveness from God, as well as from those who may have been hurt by our words or actions. Finally, we're motivated to never do it again. We're committed to learning from what happened, growing beyond it, and avoiding the same blunder next time.

FATHER, THANK YOU FOR COMFORTING AND LOVING ME EVEN WHEN I MESS UP. PLEASE HELP ME FORGIVE MYSELF, LEARN FROM MY MISTAKE, AND MOVE ON IN LIFE. AMEN.

When you stumble, the worst thing you can do is stay down. Remember who you are—a beloved but human child of your heavenly Father. He has promised to come to your aid, to comfort you, and to bring peace to your heart and mind. You can rely on His pardon. You can ask forgiveness of others. You can let your "bads" serve not only as a lesson for you but also as a good example of how to handle them.

It is well with my

BUTTERFLY BUSINESS

God is working in you to help you want to do

and be able to do what pleases Him.

PHILIPPIANS 2:13 NCV

From a small, plain, seemingly lifeless chrysalis emerges a bright, delicate, fluttering creature. Designed and created by our heavenly Father, the butterfly symbolizes His gift of renewal, resurrection, hope, and transformation.

At times in your spiritual life, you might feel trapped by layers of inertia, sluggishness, and God-silence, with little or no observable progress in conquering outside temptations or overcoming personal challenges. No brilliant "aha!" moments of sudden clarity, certainty, and understanding in matters of the spirit and no instant realization of God's presence in your life. The transformation you expected when you started on this journey has yet to take place. Is something wrong? Not at all.

God in His wisdom chooses the way of the butterfly for spiritual growth to take place. Though largely unseen even by you, His Spirit is working within you to nurture your faith. In time— God's time—you will begin to discern glimmers of comprehension and act on them. In time—God's time—you will emerge from your chrysalis, strong and trusting enough to sail on the uplifting winds of faith, hope, and love.

FATHER, STRENGTHEN MY HOPE AND READY MY SOUL FOR EVERY PURPOSE YOU'VE WRITTEN FOR MY LIFE.

ZEST FOR LIFE

Don't burn out;

keep yourselves fueled and aflame.

ROMANS 12:11 THE MESSAGE

Most kids are naturally interested, curious, and discovery-focused. They delight in learning new facts about the world, expanding their knowledge, and advancing their abilities. When they master a skill, whether simple or advanced, they beam with earned pride. Kids have enthusiasm to spare!

As the years pass, however, all too often enthusiasm fades. It gets undermined by worry and anxiety. It gets buried under a blasé facade, a seen-it-all air designed to convey urbanity and sophistication. But did you know that a vibrant, lively, living relationship with God is fueled by enthusiasm? An enthusiastic acceptance of His goodwill for you. An enthusiastic desire to build and strengthen your relationship with Him. An enthusiastic embrace of your life every new day.

Reenergize your enthusiasm for God and godliness. Take a cue from kids: explore, discover, learn, create. Join a Bible study to further explore Scripture and its application to your life. Spend time outdoors, appreciating the beauty of God's creation. Most of all, surround yourself with enthusiastic people (especially kids), because enthusiasm is delightfully contagious. Catch it and pass it on!

LORD,
HELP ME NOT TO
BURN OUT
BUT TO LIVE EACH DAY
IN AWE OF YOU
AND THE WORLD
YOU CREATED.

CONNECTION

Rejoice with those who rejoice,

and weep with those who weep.

ROMANS 12:15 NASB

God asks us to meet people where they are. Don't try to change them, fix them, or correct them, but instead recognize where they are in that very moment. Meet them in their greatest joy or their deepest pain and during times when words simply will not form in your mouth. Then just acknowledge, "I don't know what to say to you right now, but what I do know is that I want to be here for you." When you are able to say that to another human being, they immediately feel connected to you, understood by you, and less alone.

God has His own version of "meeting people where they are," and it's found in Romans 12:15 (NASB): "Rejoice with those who rejoice, and weep with those who weep." How beautiful, how perfect, how just like God! This extraordinary passage of Scripture implies that if there is reason to celebrate, then celebrate and celebrate wildly. And if there is reason for weeping, then weep and weep deeply. God is the creator and author of all emotions, and they are meant to be felt and expressed both separately as individuals and together in relationships.

GOD, HELP ME CONNECT WITH THE EMOTIONS OF OTHER PEOPLE IN ORDER TO MEET THEM WHERE THEY ARE.

REJOICE WITH THOSE WHO REJOICE, AND

weep with those who weep.

ROMANS 12:15 NASB

SELF-TALK

Be an example to the believers with
your words, your actions, your love,
your faith, and your pure life.

I TIMOTHY 4:12 NCV

*I*f you want to keep your friends, you're not likely to hurl hurtful words at them, dismiss their opinions, or ride roughshod over their feelings. Yet when it comes to one of the closest friends you have—yourself—are you also careful and considerate? Name-calling hurts others and will hurt you too.

Just as when you're talking with other people, constructive criticism you aim at yourself spurs positive change. A clear-eyed and rational assessment of what went wrong leads you to realistic, practical steps you can take toward improvement. Lesson learned? God's forgiveness prayerfully requested and fully accepted? Now leave the incident behind. Congratulate yourself, because you're willing and able to take responsibility for your actions. As of today, you know a little bit more about how to navigate the world in accordance with God's goodwill.

Listen to the words you tell yourself. Are they kindly chosen, constructive, and godly phrases and expressions? Do they build up, cheer up, and lift up? Do they leave you feeling at peace with yourself and with the desire to honor and respect yourself as someone God loves? If so, keep talking!

THANK YOU, LORD, FOR LOVING ME NO MATTER WHAT. HELP ME TO SPEAK KIND WORDS TO MYSELF—ONES THAT WILL GIVE ME THE CONFIDENCE I NEED TO LIVE MY LIFE IN YOUR LIGHT.

LOVE SONGS

The LORD your God is in your midst....
He will be quiet in His love,
He will rejoice over you with shouts of joy.

ZEPHANIAH 3:17 NASB

The second your all-time, hands-down, favorite love song comes on, your heart rate speeds up. Without a thought, you probably crank up the volume and let the music and melody take you to that special place in your mind that it always does. Through those notes and lyrics, you imagine another place and time where you soaked up the affection and attraction of someone, a place where you were free to be fully loved as the quirky and unique person you are. For three minutes, you are in your perfect paradise.

Of course, when the song ends, the day's realities resume. Romantic notions of hope and deep connection get shelved for another day. Experience tells us that even the best, most enduring love might not last, at least not with the same unbridled passion of our youth. In real life we have to settle for a love that's more down to earth and less musical. Or do we?

That's the problem with an earthbound love. We were made for more. We were designed to know and be known in the deepest levels of our soul. The God who created you sings love songs over you, rivals none. He alone can satisfy our aching souls with the kind of connection we all truly crave. Unlike love songs, God's singing for you started before He made the world, and His delight in you doesn't fade away. It welcomes you to stay in His presence and revel in His love now and forever.

LORD, SING OVER ME FOREVER! THANK YOU FOR LOVING ME AS IF I AM THE ONLY PERSON ON EARTH. HELP ME TO LOVE AS YOU LOVE.

LOVED AND LOVING

He heals the brokenhearted

and bandages their wounds.

PSALM 147:3 NCV

For broken hearts, love rarely returns easily. Protective layers of distrust, wariness, and suspicion form around the heart, shielding its tender center from further pain and hurt. Just as a scab develops over a wound, the heart's covering allows it to heal in its own time.

It could have been the passing of a loved one, the breakdown of a relationship, the betrayal of a friend . . . . Perhaps the death of a beloved pet, the loss of a career, the ending of a dream, or the memory of what once was. All hearts mourn, and not one of us can fully measure the depth of another's sorrow. Yet, as with wounds of the body, wounds of the heart are meant to heal. And God, the Great Physician, is the One whose comfort and consolation makes healing possible.

Thank God for all that love gave you and the memories it brought you, and then open your heart again. Let the gentle affection of another person, the pleading eyes of a furry friend, the lure of a new interest or intriguing idea capture your attention. Give yourself the God-created gift of loving and being loved in return.

LORD, THANK YOU FOR COMFORTING ME THROUGH THE DIFFICULT TIMES IN MY LIFE. I ASK FOR YOUR PEACE AND REST AS YOU WRAP ME IN YOUR LOVING ARMS TODAY AND FOREVER.

SAKURA BLOOMS

All people are like the grass, and all their glory is like the flowers of the field. The grass dies and the flowers fall, but the word of the Lord will live forever.

I PETER 1:24–25 NCV

It's early April, and already the delicate pink blooms of the sakura, Japanese cherry trees, have burst into billowy color. Tens of thousands of tourists have converged on our nation's capital, eager to see the softness of willowy beauty amid somber stone memorials. The landscape does not disappoint. For a brief couple of weeks, the city grounds are awash in pastel glory, the cherry blossoms accentuating the noble and heroic feats of all the lives lived and lost for a cause greater than themselves.

And then, just like that, the glory fades. The petals fall, and the world moves on. The transient display of the beautiful sakura trees tell a story just as profound as the words and historical scenes that populate the city: Even the greatest leaders do not lead forever. Soldiers, prisoners, civilians, and politicians flourish or flounder in the brevity of their lives. They, like all of us, are here today but gone tomorrow. Those who lived for something greater than themselves, however, left a lasting legacy for those coming behind. A life lived with the joy of heaven in mind brings lasting impact here on earth. God's Word alone will stand the test of time, as will all those who base their faith and actions on it.

Today, may the sobering thought of life's inevitable brevity make you bold. There's no time to waste. Live life to its fullest with God and His eternal riches in view as you ask Him to establish His order for your day.

JESUS, THANK YOU FOR THE PROMISE OF ETERNAL LIFE WITH YOU. I WANT TO LEAVE A LASTING LEGACY THAT WILL IMPACT THE WORLD FOR BETTER AND BUILD YOUR KINGDOM. BE IN MY HEART, HEAD, AND ACTIONS AS I MAKE DECISIONS FOR MY LIFE. IT'S ALL FOR YOU. AMEN.

SUN-KISSED SOULS

In the heavens God has pitched a tent for the sun....
It rises at one end of the heavens and makes its circuit
to the other; nothing is deprived of its warmth.

PSALM 19:4, 6 NIV

Have you ever encountered a blustery day when you were determined to take a walk? Dressed in gloves and what you thought would be warm clothes, you had to acknowledge your miscalculation. Coldness like liquid seeped through your clothes, chilling your skin, sending shivers all over. Goosebumps sprang up on your arms and legs despite your determined pace. But like the waters of the Red Sea, when the overhead clouds blew apart and revealed beautiful blue skies beyond, instantly things changed. The sun in all its golden glory stepped out of hiding and showered your body with unbelievable warmth. The painful chill melted under its glow, and your clothes and skin absorbed the welcome warmth. How grateful are you, in those kinds of moments, for the gift that is God's sun? Can you imagine what our world would be like without warmth? It's one of those wonders we can't live without yet is often overlooked in our day-to-day lives.

GOD, I WANT TO SOAK IN YOUR PRESENCE. LET IT WASH ME IN A WARMTH THAT YOU CAN SHARE WITH EVERYONE YOU BRING ACROSS MY PATH TODAY.

Love functions in a similar way. The pleasure of true fellowship and communion with others fills our heart with life-giving warmth. But even our earthly relationships are rays of hope sent from above. The true source of love and light and eternal warmth comes from the Father above. His presence in and through us brings meaning, hope, and the energy needed to persevere through whatever He lays before us.

GOD'S NATURE

look to the LORD and His strength;

seek His face always.

1 CHRONICLES 16:11 NIV

It was his little girl's favorite game. Every time they went on a family walk through the woods, Dad would issue his challenge: a nickel for every neat nature surprise she could find, and a whole quarter for the coolest discoveries (think lizards, frogs, snakes—anything living). She loved it! Every walk became an amazing adventure, her senses fine-tuned and focused on every unusual motion, color, or sound that could potentially score more reward. In the end, she cashed in her points at the ice cream shop, where she and her dad remembered all the wonderful scenes they had experienced together.

God doesn't want the adventure game to end as we grow up. As our loving Father, He continues to lead each of us daily on the wildest journey of our lives. When we learn to pay attention as to how God is working all around us, a whole new world of wonder and awe unfolds before our eyes. Suddenly our conversation with the cashier becomes a life-changing encounter. The wildflower springing up from within the cracked sidewalk is a sign that God's loving nature is everywhere we go. As we keep our eyes peeled for God's purpose—even in the mundane moments—we find a million beautiful miracles right around us. Joy and peace and purpose are ours every step of the way as we watch with anticipation to see God's goodness in all its glorious forms and then celebrate what we see in sweet praise to Him.

DEAR GOD, THANK YOU FOR CREATING SUCH A WONDERFUL WORLD. HELP ME SEE YOUR LOVE IN EVERY MOMENT AND KEEP MY MIND ON THINGS ABOVE INSTEAD OF WHAT MIGHT BE PHYSICALLY IN FRONT OF ME. AMEN.

IT IS FINISHED

I am certain that God, who began the good work within you, will continue His work until it is finally finished on the day when Christ Jesus returns.

PHILIPPIANS 1:6 NLT

When we work for weeks or months, even, on something creative, we are never sure whether it will work out. It begins with an idea, an inspiration to create a work of art we hope will be perfect. Then we assemble all the right tools and materials to make the vision come to life. Over time idea connects to idea, and the vision becomes reality. But that feeling of deep satisfaction we get when we stand back and see the finished product—that is worth it. The finished piece is our reward, confirming that our efforts were well spent.

Finishing tasks, even the smallest ones, like vacuuming a room or loading the dishwasher, brings a level of satisfaction. It's a reclaiming of order, if only for a moment, a restorative accomplishment in the middle of mundane details. But the projects that take longer to complete, even lifetimes, bring the greatest reward of all. These are the achievements worth standing ovations. You are a great work of art in process. Before you were born, He planned exactly where He would place you in this world. If you woke up this morning frustrated by your failures, remember that your life is not yet complete. The Master Designer is strategically crafting every moment of your life, shaping your character into one that matches the perfection in His mind. So do not worry: He has promised to finish the work He has begun, yielding His glory through you along the way.

> LORD, I AM YOUR WORKMANSHIP, CREATED IN CHRIST JESUS FOR GOOD THINGS. SHAPE ME. MOLD ME. COMPLETE IN ME YOUR PLAN FOR MY LIFE.

THE GIFT OF WATER

With joy you will draw water
from the wells of salvation.

ISAIAH 12:3 NIV

Over 70 percent of the earth's surface is covered with water. And about 60 percent of a human adult body is composed of it. It is essential to our survival. A human being can live around three weeks without food but perish in less than a week without water.

God uses water to protect. It flows throughout Scripture. God parted the Red Sea for the Israelites so that they could escape Pharaoh's army (Exodus 14:21–31). He used water to purify, deliver, and destroy in the time of Noah (Genesis 6:17). He also used water to heal, as in the story of Naaman the Syrian, who was healed from leprosy in the waters of the Jordan (II Kings 5:1–14). The Pool of Bethesda was known for annual miracles (John 5:1–9). But best of all, Jesus makes it clear that He is the Living Water. He told the woman at the well, "Everyone who drinks this water will be thirsty again, but whoever drinks the water I give them will never thirst" (John 4:13–14 NIV).

Jesus tells us that the righteous are to give drink to those who are thirsty. "I was thirsty and you gave me drink" (Matthew 25:35–40 ESV). When we offer others the gift of living water, we are offering them eternal life. "Except a man be born of water and of the Spirit, he cannot enter into the kingdom of God" (John 3:5 KJV).

THANK YOU FOR THE GIFT OF WATER, JESUS. PLEASE QUENCH MY THIRST WITH THE ETERNAL WATERS OF YOUR SPIRIT. USE ME TO DIRECT OTHERS TO THE LIFE-CHANGING LIVING WATER.

SON SHINE

The LORD appeared to us in the past, saying:
"I have loved you with an everlasting love;
I have drawn you with unfailing kindness."

JEREMIAH 31:3 NIV

As the budding young artist applied more paint to the paper on her plastic easel, she felt increasingly proud of her picture. Though each paint container held its own color, her creativity blended them all, using one brush for trunks, treetops, and flowery fields. She wondered whether anyone else in her kindergarten class was watching her wonderful masterpiece unfold. As she turned around to look for an audience, she found her teacher right behind her, beaming with pleasure. The child was elated! With more energy than ever, she returned to her work.

It's amazing what we can accomplish when the people we love believe in us. Often just a simple word of encouragement or even acknowledgment of our efforts can make all the difference in whether we forge ahead with our ideas. It's one of the reasons the apostle Paul prayed so hard for the people who had put their faith in Christ: "God, help them see just how high and deep and wide Your love for them is!" he prayed (Ephesians 3:16–18).

When we belong to Jesus, we no longer have to wonder what God thinks about us. His favor doesn't fluctuate based on how well we're drawing our picture! He's delighted that we've picked up the brush and begun applying the paint He's providing. Trust His heart and rest with confidence in His declared love for you. This world needs to see the work of art your unique personality brings to it, treasured by God every stroke along the way.

JESUS, THANK YOU FOR CHEERING ME ON AND ENCOURAGING ME AND BEING MY FRIEND. GIVE ME THE WORDS AND ACTIONS TO HELP THOSE AROUND ME FEEL LOVED AND TREASURED TOO. AMEN.

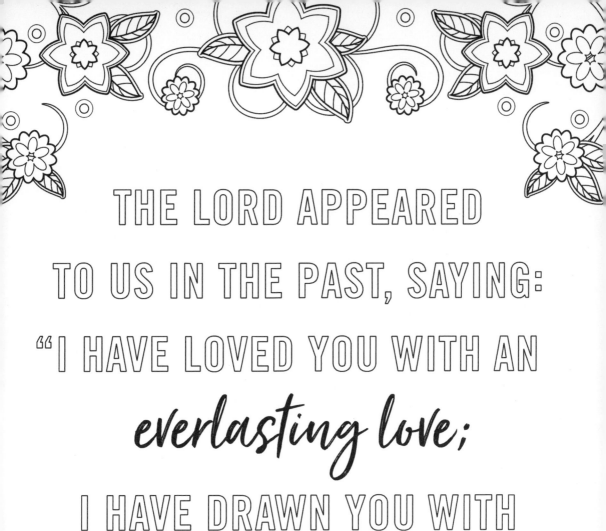

THE LORD APPEARED TO US IN THE PAST, SAYING: "I HAVE LOVED YOU WITH AN *everlasting love;* I HAVE DRAWN YOU WITH *unfailing kindness."*

JEREMIAH 31:3 NIV

TOOTING YOUR OWN HORN

Let another praise you, and not your own mouth;

a stranger, and not your own lips.

PROVERBS 27:2 ESV

Tooting one's own horn," better known as bragging, is not so much an art as a vice. "Braggadocious" offenders are everywhere—in Christmas letters, on social media, in politics, in Hollywood, on bumper stickers, on playing fields, and at weddings, funerals, and get-togethers—even in our own families. Some people rave about who they are, their accomplishments, how good they are at their jobs, their honors and awards, their academic excellence starting from kindergarten, or even how fantastic they imagine they look physically. Other people brag about what they have—their trophy wife, perfect children, designer clothing and accessories, finances, home(s), automobiles, boats, or their expensive trips and vacations. And some are super stealthy about the way they brag: "I can't believe how small the cup holders are in the new Mercedes."

The apostle Paul said we shouldn't brag about ourselves but about Christ. "As for me, may I never boast about anything except the cross of our Lord Jesus Christ. Because of that cross, my interest in this world has been crucified, and the world's interest in me has also died" (Galatians 6:14 NLT). A fool tells you what he will do, and a boaster will tell you what he has done. But a wise man does it and says nothing.

LORD, FORGIVE ME FOR BOASTING. THE NEXT TIME I WANT TO TOOT MY OWN HORN, REMIND ME THAT YOU GAVE ME THE HORN AND THE BREATH TO BLOW IT. LET THE BOAST BE ABOUT YOU AND WHAT YOU ARE DOING IN MY LIFE, NOT ME.

PRAY-TECTION

This is the confidence we have in approaching God:
that if we ask anything according to His will, He hears us.

I JOHN 5:14 NIV

*P*rayer is the wonderful way believers communicate with God. We confess our sins and tell Him our secrets, air life's hurts and frustrations, and present our requests to Him when we pray. We praise Him. We sing. We dance. And other times it's nice to just sit in the big silence that God makes when He's in the room. God doesn't need our prayers to act on our behalf; He requires them.

Scripture calls for us to pray for those who persecute us (Matthew 5:44), to "pray in the Spirit on all occasions with all kinds of prayers and requests" (Ephesians 6:18 NIV), to devote ourselves to prayer, "being watchful and thankful" (Colossians 4:2 NIV), and to "pray continually" (I Thessalonians 5:17). Jesus was always going off by Himself to find a solitary place to pray.

When we pray for ourselves, our family, friends, coworkers, neighbors, our country, and our world, a calm confidence replaces the worry and anxiety in our heart. The fear that grips us is replaced by faith when we pray. Jesus saves, heals, protects, and delivers! Prayer brings God's pray-tection. Prayer brings God's provision. Prayer brings God's peace.

DEAR JESUS, I PRAISE YOU FOR SALVATION, HEALING, PROTECTION, AND DELIVERANCE. PLEASE WATCH OVER ME AND KEEP THE LINES OF COMMUNICATION OPEN AND CLEAR SO I CAN CONTINUE TO COME TO YOU WITH CONFIDENCE.

YOUR FEARLESS FUTURE

With Him on my side I'm fearless,

afraid of no one and nothing.

PSALM 27:1 THE MESSAGE

You probably don't have to think back too far in your memory to recall a time when you felt keenly aware of God's protective presence. Perhaps it was that close call on the highway or the uninvited furry animal that showed up on your afternoon walk or the surgery you dreaded but came through with flying colors. Or the time when your grief overwhelmed you but, beneath it all, you found a place of heart-deep peace and rest.

Although God is with you always, you are likely to perceive Him more intensely when you're fearful, afraid, lonely, struggling, or grieving. Yes, scary, perilous, and troubling times come! But God makes them work for you, not against you. He uses them to draw you closer to Him, to deepen your trust in Him, and to strengthen your relationship with Him. The more you discern His presence in difficult times, the less you'll worry about them happening. Your past experience convinces you that just as He was there for you then, He will be there for you now and in the future.

What have you to fear? When you are close to Him, deeply trusting in Him, and sure of your relationship with Him—absolutely nothing!

THANK YOU, GOD, FOR YOUR PROTECTION. HELP ME TRUST YOU AS I LEARN TO LET GO OF MY WORRIES AND CONCERNS AND HOLD ONTO YOUR PEACE AND ASSURANCE.

LIGHT OF THE WORLD

I am the light of the world.
Whoever follows Me will never walk in darkness,
but will have the light of life.

JOHN 8:12 NIV

We seem to appreciate light the most when the power suddenly cuts off. The darkness is truly overwhelming when fumbling around for a flashlight or candle. Those are the moments we are most likely to stub our toe on a baseboard or trip over a child's toy. Without light, we would all be stumbling about with no idea of which direction we're headed or of the dangers near us.

Jesus said that whoever walks in the darkness doesn't know where they are going. However, He promises that those who follow the "Light of the World" will not walk in darkness but have the light of life (John 8:12 ESV). God covers Himself in light as if it were a garment (Psalm 104:1–2). God's children are children of the light (John 12:36 NLT). And there is not a speck of darkness in God. In fact, darkness cannot exist in His presence. "Even the darkness is not dark to you; the night is bright as the day, for darkness is as light with you" (Psalm 139:12 ESV). Those who follow God "walk in the light as He is in the light" (I John 1:7 ESV).

Each day, from the first blush of dawn, the sun climbs higher and higher until it is at its brightest at solar noon. At that point, a vertical stick in the ground will cast no shadow. If you're tired of fumbling around in the darkness, follow the light and stick with it.

JESUS, I'M TIRED OF FUMBLING AROUND IN THE DARK. ILLUMINATE MY PATH: PUT ME IN THE LIGHT AS YOU ARE IN THE LIGHT. BATHE ME SO FULLY IN YOUR LIGHT THAT OTHERS CANNOT HELP BUT BE DRAWN TO IT.

CLEARING THE PATH TO QUIET

Quiet down before GOD, be prayerful before Him.

PSALM 37:7 THE MESSAGE

When we're encouraged to quiet down before God and be prayerful, there's a good chance it isn't our voice we need to silence but our mind. That's where the trouble starts as far as worry, anxiety, and fear go. That's why Paul said to "fix your thoughts on what is true and good and right. Think about things that are pure and lovely" (Philippians 4:8 TLB). Paul understood the mind-body connection and he knew our worries and fears could cause us to fold under pressure.

Getting our minds to quiet down before God begins with filling them up with what His Word says: "Truly my soul finds rest in God" (Psalm 62:1 NIV); "Return to your rest, my soul, for the LORD has been good to you" (Psalm 116:7 NIV); "Come to Me, all you who are weary and burdened, and I will give you rest" (Matthew 11:28 NIV).

Another way to get our mind to quiet down and rest is to pray. In prayer, we have God's ear and we learn His heart. It's a conversation that invites us to tap into our lifeline. He has time for us no matter what, He's listening to us no matter when, and He forgives and strengthens us no matter how many times we come to the throne of His amazing grace (Hebrews 4:16). We can never exhaust His mercy. And isn't that a beautiful truth to give our spirit, soul, and body the rest it needs today?

FATHER, GIVE ME STRENGTH AND WISDOM TO PULL THE NEGATIVE "WEEDS" IN MY MIND, CLEARING THE PATH FOR PEACE, REST, AND A RENEWED CONFIDENCE IN YOU.

THE GREATEST LIGHT BEARERS OF ALL

Praise Him who planted the water within the earth,

for His loving-kindness continues forever.

PSALM 136:6 TLB

God's loving-kindness poured into the oceans and carved into the mountains. It has been sprinkled in fields of wildflowers and rolled into every wave that reaches the shore. Painted into skies of blue and scattered over the darkness in billions of stars. The definition of loving-kindness is tenderness and consideration toward others. Everything God created is for the purpose of revealing His tenderness and love toward us.

How would the world be affected if we made loving-kindness our goal? If we filtered everything we do through the questions, "Does this look like tenderness? Is this considerate of others?" It sounds like a lot of looking past ourselves and investing in everyone around us; it looks like setting our mind on things above instead of on ourselves. God has given us all of creation to see it clearly. Everything God created is part of who He is, and every part of creation is a beautiful reflection of His love. Because we're created in His image, we are the greatest light bearers of all. We are called to be careful with one another. Loving God with our whole heart means loving when it's hard to do, being kind when our patience is gone, showing tenderness in a tough situation, and putting others first when it's the last thing we feel they deserve. Kindness makes a way for God's love to have its way in the hearts that need it most.

FATHER, LET YOUR LOVINGKINDNESS COME THROUGH IN EVERYTHING I SAY AND DO TODAY. HELP ME BE ALL THAT LOVE SHOULD BE.

LIONHEART

The Spirit God gave us does not make us timid,

but gives us power, love and self-discipline.

II TIMOTHY 1:7 NIV

You could say she was a closet pray-er. Daily she prayed for her family, friends, and neighbors—especially the ones she knew hadn't yet surrendered to Jesus. On her knees in her bedroom, she was bold before the throne of God, asking for opportunities to share God's love with others.

But once she left the comfort of her own familiar quarters, she felt the battle begin. Out in the world where the people she prayed for lived, she felt less certain. For years she had simply blamed her inhibition on her temperament type. After all, the test profile proved that she was an introvert. So, naturally, the way she avoided conversation, especially about Christianity, was just a funny facet of the personality God had given her.

But no psychology test tells the full story for a believer. Ordinary inhibitions submit to God's supernatural power as we surrender to Him. No matter what our personality type may be, God gives us all a holy boldness when we seek His face first and fuel our faith with His truth and presence. Insecurities about our own abilities to carry out Jesus's Great Commission only open the door for God to do what we in our own strength can't.

FATHER, HELP ME TO BE AS BOLD AS A LION WHEN IT COMES TO SHARING ABOUT YOU! I WANT THE WORLD TO KNOW YOUR LOVE. AMEN.

Instead of cowering, cutting off the potential for spiritual conversation, trust God to make you as brave and as bold as a lion. As we pray and anticipate God moving, we can rest from our worries as we watch God make bold evangelists out of us all.

COME AS YOU ARE

If anyone thinks that he is something
when he is nothing, he deceives himself.

GALATIANS 6:3 NASB

You receive an invitation to a get-together with friends. You may ask the host, "What can I bring?" Or when you have your eye on a plum position at work, you'll ask yourself: *What skills or experience do I have that I can bring to this job?* You want to arrive at the host's home with something in your hands and at the interviewer's office with something on your resume!

With God, it's different. He urges us to come with nothing in our hands. After all, what can we give Him that He hasn't created? Don't bother to list your qualifications, either. Anything you have accomplished is His gift to you rather than your gift to Him.

God invites you to approach Him free of anything that would come between the two of you, such as a claim of human worthiness, personal pride, or a sense of self-importance. Nor should you let fear, shame, or guilt keep you away. The emptier your hands and heart, the easier it is for you to receive His gifts of comfort and peace, forgiveness and love. Come, but bring nothing. Come as you are.

FATHER, THANK YOU FOR LOVING ME SO MUCH THAT YOU ALLOW ME TO COME TO YOU WITH NOTHING AND WALK AWAY WITH EVERYTHING.

REST RESTORED

I will restore to you the years that the swarming locust has eaten....
You shall eat in plenty and be satisfied, and praise the name
of the LORD your God, who has dealt wondrously with you.

JOEL 2:25–26 ESV

Her daughter wanted to plant a garden. So the two took a trip to the local nursery, picked out pots, seeds, shovels, and fertilizer, then formed a plan as they weeded, prepped, and planted their garden. They worked in their garden for hours in the hot spring sun, digging holes and putting in seeds until darkness took over. But in the morning, they woke up to disappointment. Intrigued by the activity, their dog had dug up all they had planted. The yard was a ruined mess, the destruction seemingly beyond repair.

Sometimes we experience life like that garden. We put in the hard work of parenting or preparing for a long-held dream, only to wake up years down the road feeling as if our plans were ruined, utterly destroying our hope.

But in Jesus, hope always grows. Though our garden may no longer look like the pattern we planned, God's Word promises to bear fruit—even in the unlikeliest places—when we stay surrendered to Him. Wayward children often return home and dreams rerouted by devastating roadblocks wind up working out after all under God's sovereign plan.

When reflections on the past bring regret, remember that God restores ALL things. Nothing remains broken in His hands. He is the Master Gardener who tills our soul's soil and sends the rain for our nourishment, though we'd rather it stay sunny all the time. Waiting and trusting in His way, we'll witness the growth of a richer faith—with roots winding deeper into His love.

LORD, THANK YOU FOR RESTORING AND RENEWING ME SO THAT NOTHING CAN STOP ME FROM BRINGING YOU GLORY. AMEN.

CALMING WORDS

Have I not commanded you? Be strong and courageous.
Do not be afraid; do not be discouraged,
for the LORD your God will be with you wherever you go.

JOSHUA 1:9 NIV

She woke up with a feeling of dread. The day had finally arrived. No amount of planning or plotting could stall the inevitable any longer—and she wondered how she'd even make it out of bed, let alone face all that she knew lay ahead.

But as the early morning light slowly peeked through her shades, another thought dawned and she picked up her Bible beside the bed. There, in the pages of God's Word, she saw the promise. Written in red, Jesus's words proclaimed, "Surely I am with you always, to the very end of the age" (Matthew 28:20 NIV).

What a promise! No matter what kind of darkness threatens to undo us, we live with the promise that God never leaves us. As Jesus demonstrated to His disciples, He remains calm and completely in control of even the wildest storms. When we believe in God's goodness and power to save, our souls settle into rest with Him as we wait for His authoritative Word to have its way in our harrowing moments. Every turbulent time is an amazing opportunity to see how our Savior is mighty enough to save—*even in this*. Without the storm, we'd never experience His life-changing presence in its midst.

Instead of dreading your darkest hours or demanding that they end, draw closer to the Lord. Take pleasure in His presence and authority over your situation, and enter His rest knowing that you are safest by His side.

FATHER, THANK YOU FOR CALMING MY SOUL AND GIVING ME TRUE REST. AMEN.

LIFE LIGHT

*When Jesus spoke again to the people, He said,
"I am the light of the world. Whoever follows Me
will never walk in darkness, but will have the light of life."*

JOHN 8:12 NIV

They had sent for help long before Lazarus breathed his last breath. The sisters watched their brother's life ebb away, wondering all the while, *Where is Jesus?*

Four days Lazarus lay in the grave, rotting. It was all ruined. It's no wonder Mary didn't come running when she heard that her Lord had finally arrived in town. But Martha did, greeting him at the village gate. Full of questions, she stopped short at His. "I am the resurrection and the life," Jesus declared (John 11:25 NIV). "Do you believe this?"

Had she heard the Rabbi right? Did this man before her really have the power to resurrect the dead? Though her mind answered in the affirmative, Jesus continued His path to her heart. "Show me where your hope died," He prompted. "If you believe, you'll see God's glory there" (John 11:25–27 paraphrased).

Practical Martha protested. "He's too far gone now, Lord. The dead just stink too much!" (John 11:39 paraphrased).

Her perception didn't fully estimate God's power. Pushing past the mourning people with tears of His own streaming down His face, Jesus looked at the sealed grave. Then He shouted, "Lazarus, come forth!" (John 11:43 NKJV). As Lazarus obeyed, hope was reborn, the now-empty tomb an unquestionable triumph. Seeing became true believing, and their hearts rejoiced with hope.

LORD, THANK YOU FOR TAKING ME FROM PLACES OF DESPAIR TO WITNESSING THE WONDERS OF YOUR POWER AND LOVE.

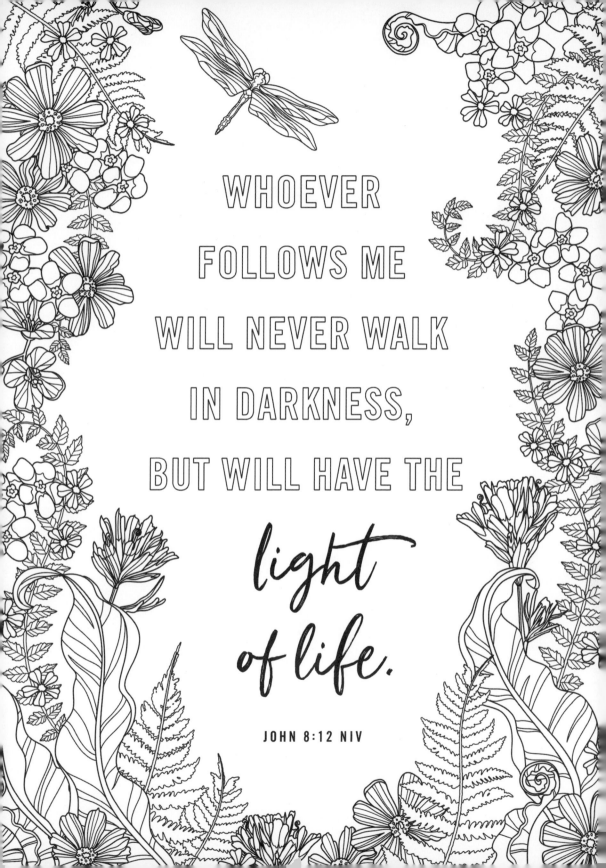

GOLDEN GOODNESS

How sweet your words taste to me;

they are sweeter than honey.

PSALM 119:103 NLT

Would you travel 55,000 miles for a pound of honey? Probably not. But a nest of foraging honeybees would put in that kind of work to produce the sweet treat. Each forager bee leaves the hive daily to collect nectar from at least one hundred flowers before returning home. With their honey tummies full, they fly back to the hive and deposit their golden goodness into hexagonal-shaped honeycomb chambers, capping them with a layer of wax when full. In this way, they have plenty of food stored up for future seasons when winter looms and blooms are scarce. Altogether, it takes more than five hundred bees visiting more than two million flowers to create one pound of honey.

Would you ever have imagined how much work went into that tiny teaspoon of honey you dab on your toast or swirl in your tea? If you put it straight on your tongue, you know it's a true golden treasure, the kind of treat only God could mastermind.

It's no wonder, then, that the psalmist compares God's Word to the sweetness of honey. The Bible you hold in your hands every day is no ordinary book. It is a miracle of God, the single sweet message of saving grace spoken by God through the pens of ordinary people over the course of more than a thousand years. "The laws of the LORD are true . . . They are sweeter than honey, even honey dripping from the comb" (Psalm 19:9–10 NLT). Savor the sweetness of God's truth and love and thank Him for all the extravagant measures He took to bring the truth to your heart.

HEAVENLY FATHER, THANK YOU FOR THE SWEETNESS OF YOUR WORD.

JESUS LOVES ME

Greater love has no one than this:
to lay down one's life for one's friends.

JOHN 15:13 NIV

If you grew up in church, you definitely grew up singing "Jesus Loves Me." The popular song sweetly sung by little children is from a Christian hymn written by Anna Bartlett Warner (1827–1915), but the lyrics first appeared as a poem in her sister Susan's novel *Say and Seal*. In the novel, the "Jesus Loves Me" verses offer comfort to a dying child. In 1862, William Batchelder Bradbury added a tune and a chorus, "Yes, Jesus Loves Me," and the song became one of the most recognizable and popular Christian hymns worldwide. Though many believers know the song inside and out, how is it that we can so easily forget the song's simple message? Children believe because the Bible tells them about the love of Christ. They know that they belong to God. They know that even though they are small, their God is big and strong and can do anything!

Faith is being sure of what we hope for and certain of what we do not see. A humble and unpretentious faith is the childlike faith Jesus tells us about. "Truly I tell you, anyone who will not receive the kingdom of God like a little child will never enter it" (Luke 18:17 NIV). Without faith, it is impossible to please God, but most important of all, without faith we cannot have Jesus in our hearts, for by faith we believe (Hebrews 11:1–6).

JESUS, FILL MY HEART WITH CHILDLIKE FAITH. I KNOW YOU LOVE ME— THE BIBLE TELLS ME SO. BUILD MY FAITH SO THAT I NEVER DOUBT IT.

AN ORDINARY WAY TO SEE OUR EXTRAORDINARY VALUE

Break open Your words, let the light shine out,
let ordinary people see the meaning.

PSALM 119:130 THE MESSAGE

We tend to complicate things. We overthink, over-worry, and overtake until we're *overwhelmed*. We can convince ourselves that being in control is comforting. In truth, it only brings a temporary sense of security. God's Word shows a different way of living in a short parable, which allows us to see that the *best* way is to go to our heavenly Father with every need. "Look at the birds of the air; they do not sow or reap or store away in barns, and yet your heavenly Father feeds them. Are you not much more valuable than they?" (Matthew 6:26 NIV).

No creation on earth is more valuable to the heavenly Father than *you*. It's as simple and as significant as that. Every moment we spend striving to get a desired outcome, every ounce of energy we exert in trying to make our lives look perfect, and every day we don't put our absolute trust in God is time we spend forgetting the simple words of our faithful Father.

Everything we have in front of us today—the people we love, our job, the chance meeting, the unexpected interruptions—is seen by the One who promises to provide every single thing we need to get through each day. We never have to wonder how we're going to handle what God allows. Our value to Him puts our life in the center of His love and at the center of His attention. His loving response is to be a Father who never forgets the extraordinary price He paid for His most valuable creation: you!

DEAR FATHER, YOUR FAITHFULNESS IS MY SECURITY IN AN UNSURE WORLD FILLED WITH UNEXPECTED CHALLENGES. I SURRENDER MY DAY TO YOU AND YOUR LOVING, ALWAYS-SUFFICIENT GRACE. AMEN.

DaySpring

LIVE YOUR FAITH

Dear Friend,

This book was prayerfully crafted with you, the reader, in mind. Every word, every sentence, every page was thoughtfully written, designed, and packaged to encourage you—right where you are this very moment. At DaySpring, our vision is to see every person experience the life-changing message of God's love. So, as we worked through rough drafts, design changes, edits, and details, we prayed for you to deeply experience His unfailing love, indescribable peace, and pure joy. It is our sincere hope that through these Truth-filled pages your heart will be blessed, knowing that God cares about you—your desires and disappointments, your challenges and dreams.

He knows. He cares. He loves you unconditionally.

BLESSINGS!

THE DAYSPRING BOOK TEAM

Additional copies of this book and
other DaySpring titles can be purchased
at fine retailers everywhere.
Order online at <u>dayspring.com</u>
or
by phone at 1-877-751-4347